PAR
2

GOLF SHORTS

1,001 OF THE GAME'S FUNNIEST ONE-LINERS

GLENN LIEBMAN

CB
CONTEMPORARY BOOKS

Library of Congress Cataloging-in-Publication Data

Liebman, Glenn.
    Golf shorts, par 2 : 1,001 of the game's funniest one-liners / Glenn
Liebman.
       p.   cm.
    ISBN 0-8092-2865-3
    1. Golf—Quotations, maxims, etc.   2. Golf—Humor.   I. Title.
GV967.L443   1997
796.352′02′07—dc21   98-12750
                                                 CIP

Jacket illustration copyright © Mark Anderson
Jacket design by Todd Petersen

Published by Contemporary Books
A division of NTC/Contemporary Publishing Group, Inc.
4255 West Touhy Avenue, Lincolnwood (Chicago), Illinois 60712-1975 U.S.A.
Copyright © 1998 by Glenn Liebman
Printed in the United States of America
International Standard Book Number: 0-8092-2865-3

00 01 02 03 04 BR 22 21 20 19 18 17 16 15 14 13 12 11 10 9 8 7 6 5 4

To my son, Franklin,
who makes every day
a wondrous journey

ACKNOWLEDGMENTS

I would like to thank the wonderful people I work with at Contemporary Books, especially John Nolan and my good friend through all ten books, Craig Bolt. Thanks as always to my agent, Philip Spitzer.

I'd also like to thank my close friend Mike Ferracane. Not only is he a great guy, but he knows more about computers than anyone this side of Bill Gates. I'd also like to thank Alan, Jessica, and Alexandra Richer, who continue to be my best customers. Alan is a one-man pro bono public relations firm.

Thanks also to my accountant, Richard Friedman. If he is as good a golfer as he is an accountant, his handicap must be incredibly low.

Special thanks also to the folks who have to put up with my whining every day at work: Adeline Quay, Doug Cooper, Sherry Campman, Ruth Foster, and Erin Barone. It is a pleasure to work alongside such dedicated, talented, and decent people.

As I have for the last nine books, I would also like to thank my family: my mother-in-law, Helen, who has a heart of gold, especially when it comes to her grandson Frankie; my brothers-in-law, Chris and Bob; my sisters-in-law, Bridget, Laura, Sharon, Deb, and Nancy; and my nieces Aimee, Samantha, and Joy (the latter two being future stars of the next Broadway revival of *The Sound of Music*).

Special thanks as always to my dad, Bernie, who taught me about perseverance and generosity toward family; my late mom, Frieda, who taught me about smiling through adversity, love of family, and generosity toward others; and my brother, Bennett, who taught me to read the racing form. Seriously, no one could have a better brother than I do.

I'd like to thank my son, Frankie, who has already developed quite a golf game. Last month he had an eagle on a course in Pennsylvania. Who cares that it was at a miniature golf course? That's still impressive for a three-year-old. Whether he's Luke Skywalker (Lucas Bucas), Batman, Robin, Little Foot, or Mr. Freeze, he is the greatest kid in the world.

Finally, thanks to the person who makes all the good things possible: my wife, Kathy. She is my best friend and the greatest person I know. I am lucky she continues to put up with my occasional forgetfulness and my inability to pick up dirty clothes.

INTRODUCTION

Of all the sports quote books I have worked on in
the last several years, none has surprised me more
than *Golf Shorts*. When I put that book together
four years ago, I found out much to my surprise
that Lee Trevino and Chi Chi Rodriguez were not
the only funny golfers. There were and are a host of
humorous golfers from the distant past (Walter
Hagen, for example), the recent past (Sam Snead),
and the present (Gary McCord, Peter Jacobsen, and
Laura Davies—to name just a few).

   This book is a tribute to the sparkling wit of
the golfing immortals as well as those mere mortals
who played the game or attempted to play the game
(such as Bob Hope and virtually every twentieth-
century president).

   So relax, kick back, and don't think about the
three-footer you just missed for par. Instead, laugh
along with golf's funniest one-liners.

"I was on the golf team for two semesters and in school for five minutes."

> *John Huston, on his college years at Auburn University*

"Golf."

> *Doug Sanders, asked his major in college*

"Sure I went to college. I delivered Christmas trees to SMU."

> *Lee Trevino, asked if he went to college*

"There aren't too many frat parties out on tour."

> *Tiger Woods, on why he was reluctant to leave college and join the pros*

"How about Byron Nelson winning the Byron Nelson?"

> *Skip Bayless, columnist, on Jack*
> *Nicklaus winning the Masters at*
> *age 46 and Ray Floyd winning the*
> *U.S. Open at age 43*

"Then I was skinnier, I hit it better. I putted better and I could see better. Other than that, everything's the same."

> *Homero Blancas, on the Senior Tour*
> *versus his younger days*

"It's a little like sex. One bad performance and you begin to wonder."

> *Julius Boros, on losing confidence in*
> *his golf game at age 55*

"Anyone who says he plays better at 55 than he did at 25 wasn't very good at 25."

> *Bob Brue*

"I'm afraid the old man has had it."

> *Jimmy Demaret, at age 47, after*
> *losing his lead at the U.S. Open on*
> *the 15th hole of the final round*

"No, I don't go places for sentiment—I have that at home. I came here believing I had a chance . . . to win."

> *Ben Hogan, asked at age 53*
> *if he came to the Masters for*
> *sentimental reasons*

"It gets easier as you get older."

> *Joe Jimenez, Senior Tour player, on*
> *shooting his age*

"I'm not sure. I think it's 27."

> *Rives McBee, asked his age, after*
> *shooting a 64 in the second round of*
> *the U.S. Open in 1966*

"The only thing I like about that number is that it's a good score to turn in for nine holes."

> *Liselotte Neumann, member of the*
> *LPGA Tour, on turning 30*

"The older you get, the stronger the wind gets—and it's always in your face."
Jack Nicklaus

"When I was growing up, they had just found radio."
Arnold Palmer, asked if he watched sports on television when he was growing up

"It's a lot nicer looking down on the grass instead of looking up at it."
Arnold Palmer, on playing in his 43rd Masters

"When you get older, your body is supposed to go. Mine is finally starting to come. I've been waiting 21 years for my body to come, and finally it's here."
Chi Chi Rodriguez, at age 45

"I guess I'm getting too old, but it took a long time for them to catch up with me."
Sam Snead, at age 64

"I used to go to the bar when I finished a round. The kids today go back and practice."
Lee Trevino

"I've gone to old addresses before—forgot that I moved."
Lee Trevino, on getting old and forgetful

"The old fellas can still win."
Lee Trevino, after Jack Nicklaus won the Masters at age 46

"It just shows this old bottle of wine hasn't turned to vinegar yet."
Tom Watson, on winning the Dunlop Open in Japan at age 48

"The young guys today play golf, go to the hotel, have an iced tea. It's a terrible way to live."
Fuzzy Zoeller

ADVICE AND CONSENT

"If I can give you any advice, it's don't listen to any advice."

> *Bruce Fleisher, advice to a*
> *young player*

"Stick your butt out more."

> *Sam Snead, golfing advice to*
> *President Eisenhower*

AFFAIRS OF THE HEART

"It would be a good course to have an affair on. Once you get into the trees off the fairway, no one will find you."

> *Amy Alcott, on the Pocono Manor*
> *Course in Pennsylvania*

"I have an old tattoo mark there. I want to have it taken off. It's a girl's name, not my wife's, so I want it removed."

> *Lee Trevino, asked to explain a*
> *bandage on his right forearm*

AMATEURS

"Amateurs look at history. Professionals look at the future."

Bernard Gallacher

"For most amateurs, the best wood in the bag is the pencil."

Chi Chi Rodriguez

AND AWAY WE GO

"When he gets into a trap, the sand has to get out."

Bob Hope, on Jackie Gleason hitting from a sand trap

ARNIE

"Put him three strokes behind anybody, and he believes he's the favorite."

Frank Beard, on Arnold Palmer

"My trouble is that when I was 14 years old I found out that every putt doesn't have to go in the hole. Palmer doesn't know that yet."
Gardner Dickinson

"I've always wanted to have a beer with Arnie, so I figured the Masters was as good a place as any."
Ken Green, on having a beer on the 15th hole of the Masters while being paired with Palmer

"I resisted the urge to get, shall we say, intoxicated Thursday night, because I was playing with Arnie."
Ken Green, on what it meant to be paired with Palmer for the first time

"If I ever had an eight-foot putt, and everything I owned depended upon it, I'd want Arnold Palmer to take it for me."
Bobby Jones

"When he hits the ball, the earth shakes."
Gene Littler, on Palmer

"There is only one thing worse than playing the way I am. That's not playing at all."

> *Arnold Palmer, during a slump in his mid-40s*

"Everyone used to say to me, 'Glad you won the tournament' . . . and now they say, 'Glad you made the cut.'"

> *Arnold Palmer*

"I saw him take one swing on the practice tee and I said that's the best golfer I'd ever seen. . . . That's the first time I saw a spark fly when the club hit the ball."

> *Gary Player, on the very first time he saw Palmer swing a golf club*

"What made him most special wasn't all the tournaments and awards he's won. It was his pure, unequaled love for the game."

> *Nick Price*

"You listen to all my jokes, and then you go and follow Arnie."

> *Chi Chi Rodriguez, kidding with the gallery at a Senior Tour event*

"He does it to all his clubs all the time. The man's got magic in there and always changes them."

Mike Souchak, on Palmer's tendency to fiddle with his golf clubs

AVOCATIONS

"The way he filled those 72 cavities during the last four days makes me think I may have been wrong."

Bobby Jones, after telling Dr. Cary Middlecoff that his future was in dentistry and not in golf

"I dropped one every now and then, but that just made the act more exciting."

Diane Patterson, on her job as catcher on a trapeze act, which she quit to go on the pro golf tour

AWARDS

"I thought you had to be dead to win that."
JoAnne Carner, on winning the
Bob Jones award for sportsmanship

BACK PAIN

"You've just got to be careful walking past the refrigerator."
Jim Colbert, who wears magnets on
his back to ward off back pain

"I was going to go out there and jump off the flagpole, just to show you how I can bounce back."
Fuzzy Zoeller, after saying he was
tired of being asked questions about
his back pain

"I shot a dial tone. I couldn't get a number."
> *Ben Crenshaw, on shooting a 76 in*
> *the first round of the Masters*

"I just had a bad day. . . . I know some of you
[reporters] misspell a word every now and then.
I misspelled the entire column."
> *Andy Dillard, on a third-round 79*
> *after being in early contention for*
> *the '92 U.S. Open*

"My swing got faster than a bolt of lightning.
I was making shots like my father, and he's a
12-handicapper."
> *Ken Green, on a second-round 78*
> *after a first-round 68 at the Masters*

"It's probably the most embarrassing round I ever
had, because I actually tried."
> *Ken Green, on shooting 87 in the*
> *first round of the '97 Masters*

"To make a birdie at the first hole and not make another after that, that's bad. That's nothing more than bad golf."

Tom Kite, criticizing his final round of the '85 U.S. Open

"If I'd been a baseball player, the manager would have yanked me."

Andy North, on a first-round 77 at the U.S. Open

"The golf course got in the way."

Calvin Peete, asked what went wrong after shooting an 87 at the Masters

"Some days you're the dog, other days you're the fire hydrant."

Larry Rinker, on a second-round 80, after a first-round lead at a Senior Tour event

SEVE BALLESTEROS

"Seve always develops a cough at the Ryder Cup."
Paul Azinger

"He's the most imaginative player in golf. He's never in trouble. We see him in the trees quite a lot, but that looks normal to him."

Ben Crenshaw, on Seve Ballesteros

"His intensity in training to beat America is second to none, and it's showing."

Colin Montgomerie, on Ballesteros's role as Ryder Cup coach for Europe

"Only a few people have ever done that to me: Bill Clinton, Nelson Mandela, George Bush, and Seve Ballesteros."

Greg Norman, on individuals who grab your attention when they walk into the room

BALTUSROL (NEW JERSEY)

"It may look, like George Foreman, as if it's been eating too many hamburgers and malts."

Jim Murray, on the huge size of Baltusrol

BELLERIVE
COUNTRY CLUB
(St. Louis)

"It was like a big bully, standing on a street corner and challenging the little kids to punch him in the stomach."

> *Arthur Daly, columnist for the*
> New York Times, *on the*
> *Bellerive course*

"It's no course you can sneak up on. Anyone who thinks he can get away with it is better off in the clubhouse drinking iced tea."

> *Billy Joe Patton*

BEVERAGE OF CHOICE

"If the ball had been in a Guinness bottle, I could not have brought myself to hit it."

> *Harry Bradshaw, Irish golfer who hit*
> *a ball in the 1949 British Open that*
> *was lying next to a beer bottle*

"It's been a long time between corks."

> *Tony Lema, nicknamed*
> *"Champagne Tony," on his*
> *eight-month losing streak*

"He fouled up once. He never got the bar set up in the players' lounge."

> *Lee Trevino, his only criticism of*
> *Billy Casper as captain of the 1979*
> *U.S. Ryder Cup Team*

"When it comes to my family, yes, but to golf, no. I'm just looking for a beer."

> *Lee Trevino, asked if he was*
> *emotional about his golf game*

"The fact that I've seen guys stone-cold drunk beat guys stone-cold sober tells you what kind of game golf is."

> *Fuzzy Zoeller*

"I used to go to all the bars."

> *Fuzzy Zoeller, asked after winning*
> *the '79 Masters at what local bar*
> *his friends would be celebrating*
> *his victory*

"I have never led the tour in money winnings. But I have many times in alcohol consumption."

> *Fuzzy Zoeller*

"Most of mine were doubles."

> *Fuzzy Zoeller, asked how many shots he took at a tournament*

BIRDIES

"God knew I couldn't putt, so He put me close to the hole."

> *Barbara Barrow, after winning the 1980 LPGA tournament with five birdies on the last nine holes*

"If you keep hitting the ball up there sooner or later the hole is going to get in the way."

> *Dave Marr, on Jack Nicklaus's 50-foot birdie putt*

"If you took 100 balls and pitched them by hand from there, you couldn't do any better."

> *Bill Rogers, on Tom Watson's birdie from the rough on the 17th hole at Pebble Beach that propelled him to victory in the 1982 U.S. Open*

BOGEY MAN

"You might say I bogeyed and double bogeyed with steady efficiency."

> *Ron Castillo, touring pro, on shooting 88 and 87 in the first two rounds of the '76 PGA*

"All my life I've been trying to make a hole in one. The closest I ever came was a bogey."

> *Lou Holtz*

"I couldn't care less about all those fiction stories about what happened in the year 1500 or 1600. Half of them aren't even true."

John Daly

"Half of the people I meet say, 'When did *Buried Lies* come out?' and the other half say, 'You wrote a book?'"

Peter Jacobsen, after his book Buried Lies *was published*

"How about that? I didn't think Gay had ever read a book in his life."

Bobby Nichols, on Gay Brewer crediting Dr. Norman Vincent Peale's The Power of Positive Thinking *for his Masters victory*

"If I keep playing like this, it's going to be Win to Eat."

Jack Nicklaus, after not making the cut in the U.S. Open while reading the book Eat to Win

19

PAT BRADLEY

"Death, taxes, and Pat Bradley's name on the leader board."

> *Val Skinner, LPGA pro, on the three*
> *things you can count on in life*

BRITISH OPEN

"When you're walking over a bridge that's older than your country, that makes it a special place."
> *Paul Azinger, on St. Andrews*

"It's unusual for a bad player to do so well. . . . I generally play badly."

> *Ken Brown, English pro, on*
> *being only four shots off the pace*
> *entering the final round of the 1980*
> *British Open*

"I do not think I could go on living unless I felt that one day I might win the Open Championship at St. Andrews."

> *Ben Crenshaw*

"Nearly every course has a bit of St. Andrews in it."

Ben Crenshaw

"Would I have to learn the rules and all that crap?"

John Daly, upon being asked to join the prestigious Royal and Ancient after winning the '95 British Open

"It's a beast, but just a beast."

Bernard Darwin, on Royal Lytham

"It's target golf, but here the target moves."

David Feherty, on the 20-mph winds at St. Andrews

"The worst piece of mess I have ever played."

Scott Hoch, on St. Andrews

"I love the hole. It's an honor to say I've been eaten alive by it."

Peter Jacobsen, on the famous 17th at St. Andrews

"I could take out of my life everything except my experiences at St. Andrews and I'd still have a rich, full life."

Bobby Jones

"There is always a way at St. Andrews, although it is not always the obvious way."

Bobby Jones

"One can feel so lonely at St. Andrews missing a putt."

Jack Nicklaus

"The Shark is back on the prowl and as hungry as ever."

Greg Norman, on defending his '87 British Open title

"I just miss a putt. I don't kill anybody."

Costantino Rocca, on missing an easy putt that would have likely made him winner of the '95 British Open

"As soon as I make this, I'm going to bow to the gallery."

> *Doug Sanders, just before missing a two-foot putt that would have made him the 1970 British Open champion*

"What is this old, abandoned golf course?"

> *Sam Snead, upon seeing St. Andrews for the first time*

"Anytime you leave the U.S.A., you're just camping out."

> *Sam Snead, on his British Open failures*

"The Sistine Chapel of golf."

> *Frank "Sandy" Tatum, former president of the U.S. Golf Association, on St. Andrews*

"If there is one part of your game not right, no matter how you try your hardest to protect it, the Old Course will find it."

> *Peter Thomson, on St. Andrews*

"The Open is one of the few tournaments where you can go out in a short-sleeve shirt and come in with skis on."

Lee Trevino

"I know I'm fighting the law of averages, but I've been fighting the law of averages all my life."

Lee Trevino, on the possibility of his winning the 1971 British Open after winning two tournaments in the prior three weeks (he ended up winning the Open)

"Tell them in England that Super Mex is on the way. You can tell them I'll give them hell."

Lee Trevino, on the '71 British Open

"I didn't win the championship. I had it given to me."

Tom Watson, after his competition fell apart in the final round of the '82 Open

"A nice oasis after a three-year dry spell."

Tom Watson, on winning the '80 British Open

"This tournament is what golf is all about. You cannot live golf any more than you do when you come down the 18th fairway of this golf course a champion."

Tom Watson, on Muirfield in 1980

"You don't go in there, you send your beagle in there to get something out."

*Fuzzy Zoeller, on the grass at
St. Andrews*

BROTHERLY LOVE

"After all, if you cannot trust someone named Jesus, who can you trust?"

*Chi Chi Rodriguez, on getting advice
from his brother Jesus*

"I'd like to see Bobby's name up there on the leader board with mine on Sunday, as long as his name is just below mine."

*Lanny Wadkins, during a tournament
in which he and his brother Bobby
were both close to the lead*

BUNKERS

"I wouldn't say that God couldn't have got it out of there, but He would have had to have thrown it."
Arnold Palmer, after having problems with a bunker shot

"There is no such thing as a misplaced bunker. Regardless of where a bunker may be, it is the business of a player to avoid it."
Donald Ross, legendary golf-course architect

CADDIES

"Caddies are not very smart. Most of them get 5 percent of the player's purse. In my case, Bob gets 5 percent and I take the other 95 percent."
Jane Betley, on caddying for her husband Bob

"Shelly has no clue when it comes to golf—but I can tell her things I wouldn't tell anyone else."

Ken Green, on his sister Shelly, who served as his caddie

"Between taking care of the pets and caddying for Ken, I haven't had much time for anything else."

Shelly Green, on her brother Ken bringing their pets on the road with them

"My idea of a caddie is the one I won the Masters with. Never said one word."

Claude Harmon

"The way Betsy was playing, Rin Tin Tin could carry her clubs and it wouldn't make any difference."

Gary Harrison, caddie for Betsy King, who shot 17-under to win the LPGA championship

"He's still caddying for me. He carries the bag from the trunk of the car to the golf course."

Nancy Lopez, on firing her husband, baseball player Ray Knight, as her caddie

"My feeling was that as long as he was punctual and sober, knew the rules, and was strong enough to carry the bags, he was fine with me."

Peter Thomson, on caddies

"He can make more money gettin' hit by me than by caddying."

Lee Trevino, on hitting a caddie during a practice round at the British Open

BILLY CASPER

"Casper never, never gave a tournament away. In his prime, you couldn't beat him."

Dave Marr, on Billy Casper

"He's been as invisible as you can be winning 50 tournaments."

Johnny Miller, on Casper

"Put a swimming pool in my backyard."

> *Amy Alcott, who jumped into a lake*
> *after winning the Dinah Shore*
> *Classic, asked what she would do*
> *with her $90,000 winnings*

"I was very dignified, was I not?"

> *Patty Sheehan, after winning the*
> *Dinah Shore and jumping into*
> *the water*

CHI CHI

"I know why they're so slow. Chi Chi's got all the money in his pockets."

> *Greg Norman, on Chi Chi Rodriguez*
> *being part of a slow foursome that*
> *was ahead of Norman*

"Call me a clown, call me a serious guy, call me a nice guy, just don't call me collect."

> *Chi Chi Rodriguez*

"Who do you work for, the post office?"
Chi Chi Rodriguez, to a
photographer who was taking
numerous pictures of Chi Chi

"If they put the flag in the *Titanic*, I'll go for it."
Chi Chi Rodriguez, on his
aggressive attitude

CHOKE HOLD

"Competition is even more fun than golf. I like going down to the wire knowing somebody's going to choke, and hoping it's not me."
JoAnne Carner

"You can print it now. . . . That's why Hoch rhymes with choke."
Scott Hoch, on losing a tournament
with a seven-stroke lead in the
final round

"We all choke, and the man who says he doesn't choke is lying like hell. We all leak oil."
Lee Trevino

CLASS

"I believe if society in general conducted itself the way we golfers do, this would be a much better world."

Ray Floyd

"Show us a golf-playing town and the writer will show you a town in which refinement is above the average."

Damon Runyan

"Life on the tour can be a Fantasy Island of private planes, limousines, and fancy suits in glad places. Everything but Tatoo saying, 'De plane, de plane.'"

Fuzzy Zoeller

CLOTHESHORSE

"But I'm sure as hell not going to wear knickers."
John Daly, after saying he would do virtually anything to win a tournament

"For that kind of money, I'd wear a skirt."

Jimmy Demaret, on players
complaining about having to
wear numbers while playing in
the money-laden George May
tournaments of the 1940s and '50s

"I got my ideas about colorful clothes from
watching my father mixing his paints in
the garage."

Jimmy Demaret, on his
colorful wardrobe

"I used to get my share of catcalls from the gallery,
but I just whistled right back at them."

Jimmy Demaret, on his
canary-yellow pants

"If you're going to be in the limelight, then you
might as well dress for it."

Jimmy Demaret, on his
clothes philosophy

"When you play in pink knickers, you'd better be
able to drink, play, and fight like hell."

Jim Ferree, on wearing pink knickers
on the Senior Tour

"If you see only one, you can be damn sure I've got green undies on."

> *Simon Hobday, on his superstition*
> *of always wearing two articles of*
> *green clothing*

"I'll probably come out there in some really flashy outfit. A nice bold gray and a white visor. Black shoes. Navy slacks. I'll dazzle 'em."

> *Tom Kite, asked if he had any plans*
> *to wear a gaudy outfit for the final*
> *round of the U.S. Open*

"I can't even get a pair of pants. Not even a pair of jeans."

> *Wayne Levi, touring pro, on trying to*
> *get a contract with Levi's jeans*

"Men play it in caps that look as if they have been borrowed from a guy on a tractor."

> *Jim Murray, on golf and*
> *golfers' attire*

"I love westerns, and the cowboys always looked good in black."

> *Gary Player, on why he likes*
> *wearing black*

"I'm wearing an Arnold Palmer hat made in Japan. These are Johnny Miller slacks, but I've taken the tag out."

Chi Chi Rodriguez, on his outfit at the U.S. Open

"Not orange. That's tangerine."

Doug Sanders, to a spectator commenting on his orange outfit

"Arnold Palmer likes airplanes. Jack Nicklaus likes boats. I like clothes."

Doug Sanders, on his love of clothes

"Hopefully nobody will be asking me for directions. Hopefully I'll be on the fairway so that won't happen."

Payne Stewart, known for wearing knickers, on volunteers in a tournament having to wear knickers

"How to knock a guy out in a bar."

> *JoAnne Carner, on the only thing she
> did not learn from her friend Billy
> Martin*

"All those jokers can putt or they wouldn't be out here. But since I ain't got nothing else to do, I can see when the action goes wrong—and help straighten them out."

> *George Low, legendary
> putting instructor*

"Give me a millionaire with a bad backswing and I can have a very pleasant afternoon."

> *George Low*

"Some of those coaches are nice guys, but most can't break 80."

> *Jack Nicklaus*

"My wife told me to quit giving lessons and start taking them."

> *Phil Rodgers, on working as Greg
> Norman's instructor*

COCKEYED PESSIMIST

"I'll probably shoot 85 tomorrow."

> *Charlie Coe, after shooting a*
> *first-round 71 in the '66 Masters*

"No I can't. I guess I could win if everybody else broke their leg or something."

> *Nolan Henke, asked, while he was*
> *one shot off the lead halfway through*
> *the '91 U.S. Open, if he could win*
> *the tournament*

"It never occurs to Arnold that the ball won't go in the hole, but I'm always surprised when it does."

> *Gene Littler, comparing his*
> *putting philosophy with that*
> *of Arnold Palmer*

COMMISSIONER

"A little man who wants to be big."

> *Seve Ballesteros, on former*
> *commissioner Deane Beman*

"I'm not allowed to complain for two years. It's part of my retirement package."

> *Deane Beman, on not responding to his critics after his retirement*

"He's not somebody you want to be driving cross-country with and have the car radio go out."

> *Dave Marr, on Beman*

CONGRESSIONAL CLUB (WASHINGTON, D.C.)

"Best course I ever won the Open on."

> *Ken Venturi, asked what he thought about Congressional Club after winning the 1964 U.S. Open*

CHARLES COODY

"Charlie's one of our better shotmakers, but he tries hard not to win."

> *Frank Beard, on Coody's inability to win before winning the 1971 Masters*

"I birdied the second hole and said, 'God bless you, Francis.' After I started getting bogies, I threw the flower out."

> Mac O'Grady, on visiting the Francis
> Ouimet memorial house and grabbing
> a flower before the 1988 U.S. Open
> at Country Club

"I feel as though I've been in jail for five days."

> Art Wall, on Country Club

"It has been very important for me to know where the pin placements and the Porta-Johns are."

> D. A. Weibring, on the 1986
> U.S. Open at Country Club

COURSES

"It's easier to tell a man that there is something wrong with his wife than with his golf course."

> Frank Hannigan, former executive
> director of the USGA

"You would have dead flat greens and dead flat fairways, very little rough and very few traps. That kind of course wouldn't require an architect. You could order it from a Sears Roebuck catalogue."

Robert Trent Jones, on the courses golf pros would design

BEN CRENSHAW

"He could break par blindfolded."

Anonymous, on Crenshaw's legendary putting skills

CROSBY PRO—AM

"It takes three weeks to get your swing back."

Gay Brewer, on playing at three different courses at the Crosby

"If I was asked what single thing has given me the most gratification in my long and sometimes pedestrian career, I think I would have to say it is this tournament."
Bing Crosby

CURSES, FOILED AGAIN

"I never cussed much. That's a bunch of bull——."
Tommy Bolt, on cursing

CUTS

"The only good job I've done this week is making a perfect fool of myself."
Sandy Lyle, on missing the Masters cut after winning the year before

"I missed the nine-hole cut."
Dave Marr, on shooting a 70 in an exhibition match where Nicklaus shot 66, Snead shot 64, and Boros shot 62

"I'd rather win one tournament in my entire life than make the cut every week."
Arnold Palmer

"There's only one thing worse than missing the cut in a tournament, and that's having to spend the night in the city where you missed the cut."
Joey Sindelar

JOHN DALY

"I wasn't mad. I just didn't ever want to see it again."
John Daly, on not enjoying the Scandinavian Masters

DEATH BE NOT PROUD

"When I die I want to be reincarnated as myself. I like all the things I like."
David Feherty

"I thanked them for the invitation, but I asked them to please put it off until I was dead if they want a memorial."

> *Ben Hogan, on turning down an*
> *honor at a tournament hosted by*
> *Jack Nicklaus*

"'I told you I was sick.'"

> *Lee Trevino, on how he wanted his*
> *tombstone to read*

"I'm going to die in a tournament on the golf course. They'll just throw me in a bunker and build it up a little bit."

> *Lee Trevino*

JIMMY DEMARET

"There's no telling what Jimmy would have done if he had toed the line and gone to bed at a decent hour."

> *Sam Snead, on Demaret*

"People thought that it was pretty amazing, since he did it without practicing. I thought it was even more amazing because he did it without sleeping."
Sam Snead, on Demaret winning three Masters

DO THE HUSTLE

"If a stranger with a goofy swing wants to play for more than loose change, take a pass. It's a long walk back to your hotel in bare feet."
Mike Royko

"Let's face it. I've been a hustler all my life."
Lee Trevino

DON'T NEED NO
STINKING BADGES

"I'm told the next time John Huston wins on the PGA Tour, he will be given the treasure of Sierra Madre."

Terry Boers, columnist,
Chicago Sun-Times

DRIVE MY CAR

"Your professional golfer takes longer to line up a six-foot putt than the Toyota Corporation takes to turn raw iron ore into a Corolla."

Dave Barry

"It's a coffin on wheels."

Greg Norman, on his
$130,000 Testarossa

"It caught fire when I stopped at a traffic light."

Jesper Parnevik, on why he finally
gave up his 1972 Cadillac convertible

"Golf is like driving a car. As you get older, you get more careful."
Sam Snead

DRIVES

"Finish high and let 'em fly."
Patty Berg, describing her
golfing philosophy

"Luckily it was downwind and with a lie. Otherwise, I'd be off being drug-tested."
Laura Davies, on driving a 4-iron
over 240 yards

"The difference between now and when I played during my younger days is my drives are shorter and my short game is longer."
Simon Hobday

"I hit my longest drive 250 yards. Trouble was, it was on a 175-yard par 3."
Abe Lemon, college basketball coach

"That one landed between out-of-bounds and the outhouse."

> Gary McCord, on a bad drive hit by Arnold Palmer

"Everyone wants to be known as a great striker of the ball. Nobody wants to be called a lucky, one-putting S.O.B."

> Gary Player, on the lack of emphasis put on putting

"If I could hit one that far, I'd probably be pumping gas now."

> Lee Trevino, joking with Larry Ziegler, who hit a poor drive in a practice round before the Masters

EAGLES

"We call it double eagle."

> T. C. Chen, asked to give the Chinese translation of his first-round double eagle at the 1985 U.S. Open

"The winds of adversity blew on the flame."
>   *Mac O'Grady, on his unsuccessful*
>   *early career*

"Time goes by and people forget all the tournaments I've won. Only my wife and my dog remember."
>   *Gary Player*

EGO

"Big hands, big feet, and a big head."
>   *Anonymous, on the things needed to*
>   *be a great golfer*

"Who's going to be second?"
>   *Walter Hagen, frequently said before*
>   *a tournament began*

ERNIE ELS

"I think I just played with the next God."
Curtis Strange, on Ernie Els

FAMILY AFFAIR

"After I won, I asked my wife what she wanted. She said a divorce. I said I wasn't thinking of anything that expensive."
Nick Faldo, after winning $1 million in a tournament

"This is bad for me, my kids, and my ex-wife."
Ken Green, on missing a cut at a Florida tournament

"We had one player drop out, one transfer, and one run off with Nick Faldo."
Rick LaRose, Arizona's women's golf team coach, on the team's need to start over

"You can make a lot of money in this game. Just ask my ex-wives. Both of them are so rich that neither of their husbands work."
> *Lee Trevino*

FAMILY FUN

"My wife will find ways to spend $16,000 first-prize money in 16 minutes."
> *Julius Boros, on winning the*
> *1963 U.S. Open*

"He started thinking, 'My dad's going to pass me on the money list.'"
> *Bob Duval, Senior Tour pro,*
> *explaining the motivation behind*
> *the three-tournament winning*
> *streak of his son David*

"A real live nephew of his uncle Sam."
> *Mickey Herskowitz, golf writer, on*
> *J. C. Snead, nephew of Sam Snead*

"First comes my wife and children. Next comes my profession—the law. Finally, and never as a life in itself, comes golf."

Bobby Jones

"It's hard being the father of a famous son."

Jack Nicklaus, after Jack Nicklaus II won an amateur tournament

"I haven't seen them at the family reunion yet."

Chris Patton, asked if he was related to General George Patton or golfer Billy Joe Patton

"For a long while, my son thought only women played golf."

Judy Rankin, on her son, Walter, who traveled around with her on the pro tour

"The place of the modern father in the modern suburban family is a very small one, particularly if he plays golf."

Bertrand Russell, British author

"My family was so poor, they couldn't afford any kids. The lady next door had me."

Lee Trevino

FARMER'S MARKET

"I can talk to the cows and get them to go, but that golf ball, it doesn't listen to me at all."

Robert Landers, Senior Tour player and professional farmer

"Being out in the woods is fun, but this pays better."

Robert Landers, asked if he would rather cut wood or golf

FINAL ROUNDS

"I hit some crummy shots. And when I hit some good shots, I hit crummy putts."

Rick Fehr, on his final-round 73 in the '85 U.S. Open

"I felt like a lawn mower that just wouldn't turn
over. I just couldn't get started."

> *Peter Jacobsen, on three lackluster*
> *early rounds at a tournament before*
> *a final-round 64*

"You feel alone, scared, like you're sitting on top
of the [space] shuttle and any second it could
blow up."

> *Mac O'Grady, explaining the*
> *emotions of the last round of*
> *a tournament*

"I feel like an elephant stepped on my money clip."

> *Chi Chi Rodriguez, on shooting a*
> *final-round 81 after being in*
> *contention in a tournament*

RAYMOND FLOYD

"His idea of sacrifice was to get home by sunrise."

> *Jim Murray, on the early partying*
> *years of Ray Floyd*

"He gets this look. His eyes get big and round and they seem to be staring at something you can't see."

> *Payne Stewart, on Floyd's ability to play in the clutch*

"When he sees victory, all he sees is the ball going to the next pin."

> *Lanny Wadkins, on Floyd*

FLY BY NIGHT

"I don't know what ticked them off, but they were mad as hell."

> *Keith Fergus, on being attacked by bees during a tournament*

"When your full-view focus is on the ball and an object enters your peripheral-view field of sight—that dragonfly—the object scrambles your learned motor memory system."

> *Mac O'Grady, on a dragonfly attack during the Masters*

"I just hope we can still get Oreos and Fig Newtons at the turn."

> *Paul Azinger, on Nabisco no longer sponsoring a tournament*

"It was free."

> *Seve Ballesteros, asked what he liked about the meal, a Scottish dish of oatmeal and beef, chosen the night before the Masters by previous year's champion Sandy Lyle*

"I was just trying to make a statement."

> *Lori Garbacz, after criticizing slow play on the women's tour by ordering a pizza, which arrived before she was in the clubhouse*

"You can't hurt them. You can sit on them or throw them and they still stay the same."

> *Al Geiberger, on why he eats peanut butter sandwiches during tournaments*

"They don't spoil like tuna fish would."

Al Geiberger, another reason why he
likes peanut butter sandwiches

"The only time I'll pick up a check is to hand it
to somebody."

George Low, legendary
putting instructor

"I would rather play golf than eat."

Lee Trevino

"White Castle."

Fuzzy Zoeller, asked after winning
the '79 Masters what he would
choose for next year's meal

FOREIGN INVASION

"Birdie the same, par the same, bogey the same,
out-of-bounds the same."

Seve Ballesteros, comparing the
U.S. and European tours

"What Cornwallis surrendered at Yorktown has been reclaimed by Lyle, Faldo, and Woosnam on the manicured battleground at Augusta."

> *Larry Guest,* Orlando Sentinel, *on several years of English dominance at the Masters*

FRONT—RUNNER

"It's always hard to sleep when you've got a big early lead. You just lie there and smile at the ceiling all night."

> *Dave Stockton*

"It lets me know there still is a spark in the fireplace. I just have to know where to throw the wood."

> *Lee Trevino, on a first-round 67 at the Masters at age 49*

"If I'm leading Saturday night, I may not show up. I may have a heart attack."

> *Lee Trevino, on what it would mean to win the Masters after a first-round lead*

"When you're the leader, why shoot at the pins? Make those other guys come to you."
Fuzzy Zoeller

GALLERY

"Do you mind if I play while you talk?"
Seve Ballesteros, said laughingly while playing in front of a loud gallery

"I hit it two feet from the pin on the first hole and both people clapped."
Jim Colbert, on being forced to play early in a tournament due to a scheduling conflict

"No matter what it is, even tiddledywinks, they are gonna be out there watching."
Ben Crenshaw, on New England sports fans

"He was having a few pops. I know if I was at a golf tournament spectating, I'd have a few pops, too."

Andy Dillard, on a fan vocally cheering for him early in the '92 U.S. Open

"They're more laid-back than any of the others. I always like playing in the Middle West."

Hubert Green, on galleries in the Midwest tournaments

"Unfortunately, I didn't hit balls outside the ropes, so I couldn't get out to say hello."

Ayako Okamoto, on the large number of Japanese fans cheering her in a San Diego tournament

"Maybe I cheered the gallery up a little. Watching me today, maybe they feel better about their own games."

Arnold Palmer, on shooting a 160 total in the first two rounds of the '87 Masters

"I call my crowd 'Arnie's Leftovers.'"

> *Chi Chi Rodriguez, on being second*
> *fiddle to Palmer on the Senior Tour*

"I think they got all the fools they could find and put them right here. Sounds like a baseball game."

> *Lee Trevino, on fans screaming for*
> *him at the U.S. Open*

"Those people standing behind the ropes are paying the freight. I want them to feel that if they want to ask a question they can ask one."

> *Fuzzy Zoeller, on having fun with*
> *the gallery*

GAMBLIN' MAN

"It's helped me a lot more than any pretty swing I'm supposed to have."

> *Frank Beard, on how playing for*
> *dimes and quarters early in his*
> *career made him a better golfer*

"You've got it all wrong. Golf is the biggest betting sport in the world, but it all takes place on the first tee."

Jimmy the Greek, on claims that football and basketball are the top betting sports

"We have feelings and we have egos, and it does a professional's ego no good at all to see himself dismissed as a 100-to-1 chance for a particular tournament."

Greg Norman, on British oddsmakers providing odds on who would win tournaments

"Never gamble with a stranger, and if you do and he stops arguing the handicap too soon, you know you got a hawk in the chicken yard."

Sam Snead

"I just barely lost for the day."

Fuzzy Zoeller, on winning $2,500 on the '95 Kentucky Derby

GET A GRIP

"You get rewarded at the bottom end of the club by what you do at the top end."

> *Jerry Barber, on the importance of a good grip*

GOD BLESS AMERICA

"Maybe California my place. It used to be owned by the Spanish. Maybe I get it back."

> *Seve Ballesteros, on playing well at tournaments in California*

"Right turn on a red light. I think that's brilliant."

> *Nick Faldo, on what he likes best about the United States*

"The only thing I can't do in the U.S. is vote and work for the government, but with the taxes I pay, I feel like I work for the government."

> *David Graham, from Australia, on his permanent alien-resident status*

"Nick's in a different situation. He has an American girlfriend. I don't have an American girlfriend."

> *Colin Montgomerie, on why he doesn't play in the United States as much as Nick Faldo*

"Baseball players retire, football players retire, hockey players retire, basketball players retire, then they play golf, don't they? This is the game."

> *Lee Trevino, on why golf is truly America's game*

GOLDEN BEAR

"If there's a putt to be made and the noose is around my neck, and I live or die by it, there's nobody I'd sooner have on the green for me than Jack Nicklaus."

> *Furman Bisher, columnist for the* Atlanta Constitution

"I felt it was my opportunity to prolong the legacy of Jack Nicklaus."

> *Hale Irwin, on a final-round loss to Nicklaus in a Senior Tour event resulting in Nicklaus's 100th victory*

"I think you'd have to say he's past his prime."

> *Tom Kite, said about Nicklaus four days before Jack won the '86 Masters*

"That man makes you feel sort of insuperior."

> *Johnny Miller, on being glad that he wasn't paired with Nicklaus at a tournament*

"You always want Jack Nicklaus to win golf tournaments. The way you always wanted Ruth to get homers."

> *Jim Murray*

"About on par with seeing smoke signals on the horizon or hearing drums outside the fort at night."

> *Jim Murray, on Nicklaus being in close pursuit of a competitor*

"I don't think Jack has too many problems on any kind of course."

> *Andy North, asked if Nicklaus would*
> *have problems at Shinnecock Hills*

"A definite air of electricity emanates from him. It's stronger than a nuclear reactor. The man simply never makes a mistake."

> *David Ogrin*

"I let the Bear out of the cage."

> *Arnold Palmer, on losing to Nicklaus*
> *at the '62 U.S. Open*

"That big, strong dude. I thought I was through with him yesterday."

> *Arnold Palmer, on Nicklaus staying*
> *close to Palmer at the '62 U.S. Open*

"Jack could play badly and still get the ball in the hole and win."

> *Gary Player*

"That's where a bear belongs."

> *Chi Chi Rodriguez, on Nicklaus*
> *driving a ball into the woods*

"I figured if old Jack Nicklaus could do it at 46. . . ."

> *Willie Shoemaker, on winning the*
> *Kentucky Derby at age 53 after*
> *drawing inspiration from Nicklaus's*
> *Masters victory*

"When you go head-to-head against Nicklaus, he knows he's going to beat you, you know he's going to beat you, and he knows you know he's going to beat you."

> *J. C. Snead*

"What am I supposed to say, that he's God and everybody should stay home?"

> *J. C. Snead, asked if Nicklaus was*
> *unbeatable after losing to him in*
> *a playoff*

"Hogan and Jones would have never handled him. Jack's the best ever to wear cleats and the best who ever will."

> *Lee Trevino*

"I came up in the era of the greatest player who ever played the game, and I beat him every once in a while."

Lee Trevino, on his proudest accomplishments

"If Nicklaus tells you an ant can pull a bale of hay, don't ask questions, just hook him up."

Lee Trevino

"If Jack had to play my itty-bitty tee shots, he'd have quit golf and opened a pharmacy in Ohio."

Lee Trevino

"Have a birth certificate in your pocket that says you're Jack Nicklaus."

Lee Trevino, asked the best way to play the Masters

"I'm a lucky dog. You got to be lucky to beat Jack Nicklaus—because he's the greatest golfer who ever held a club."

Lee Trevino, on beating Nicklaus in the '71 U.S. Open playoff

"The Good Lord gave Jack Nicklaus everything—and I mean everything—except a wedge. If he had given him that, the rest of us might never have won any tournaments."

Lee Trevino

"There is in him the stuff of the fantastic, the phenomenal, the likes of which may never be seen again."

P. J. Ward-Thomas, Manchester Guardian

GOLF AND BASEBALL

"My baseball would be worse than my golf, which isn't very good."

Joe DiMaggio, jokingly asked at the U.S. Open if he would make a comeback with the Yankees at age 55

"The way things have been going lately I might want Dennis Eckersley to finish up for me."

Jay Haas, on his good starts and poor finishes in tournaments

"I hit a long ball in baseball, just like in golf, but I didn't hit it often enough."

> J. C. Snead, on why he gave up
> baseball for golf

"If Ted Williams had become a golfer, I don't think the game would have seen a more positive player."

> Sam Snead

"I'd watch baseball if it was a 3–2 Little League game."

> Tom Watson, on his love for baseball

GOLF AND BOXING

"As a golfer, Tex remained a top promoter."

> Grantland Rice, on the golfing
> abilities of legendary boxing promoter
> Tex Rickard

"Doesn't he know he's supposed to go to football games in the fall?"

> *Andy Bean, on being in a tight autumn race with Bob Tway for overall point standings that guaranteed a $500,000 bonus for the winner*

"I'm very glad I gave up football, or I wouldn't be here tonight."

> *Patty Berg, reminiscing during her Hall of Fame induction ceremonies about how she excelled in football growing up*

"I was small, but I was slow."

> *Jim Colbert, on his days as a college football player*

"I guess the first time I three-putt."

> *Mike Ditka, on when he would start thinking about the following season after winning the Super Bowl*

"In football, you can get stuffed and it's second and 12 and you come up with a big play. In golf, every shot is a pressure shot."

> *Wayne Fontes, former head coach of the Detroit Lions*

"He was a great person to work for, he was a great competitor, and I could beat him in golf."

> *Lou Holtz, former Notre Dame football coach, on Gene Corrigan leaving as athletic director*

"He was the strong safety and I was the smart one."

> *Hale Irwin, on his reunion with former college teammate Dick Anderson of the Miami Dolphins*

"No, I dream of being Eddie DeBartolo. He pays Joe Montana."

> *Roger Maltbie, 49ers fan, asked if he ever dreamed of being Joe Montana*

"Every kid in Texas was either a football player or a golfer, it seemed, and some were both."

> *Dave Marr*

"My problem is I play golf like Ray Nitschke."

> *Mac O'Grady, describing his intensity on the golf course*

"The only thing I'm worried about is getting the left hand steady, then hitting it straight."

> *Lawrence Taylor, on his retirement*

"I shot a Red Grange today."

> *Tom Watson, on shooting a 77 at the U.S. Open, the uniform number of Red Grange*

GOLF AND HOCKEY

"I sliced it. Bad habit from my golf game."

> *Martin Brodeur, New Jersey Devils goalie, after almost scoring a goal while clearing the puck*

"Playing golf is like losing 14 games in a row in overtime. It's like hitting 15 goalposts."

> *John Brophy, former Maple Leafs coach who caddied for his girlfriend on the LPGA Tour*

"One of the nice things about golf is that nobody slams into you when you're in the backswing."
Pierre Larouche

"If you miss a putt, you don't have your defenseman or goalie to bail you out."
Bob Nevin, former hockey player, on the difference between hockey and golf

GOLF BALLS

"Wouldn't you pick up a dollar bill if you saw it? And golf balls cost more."
Lee Trevino, on picking up four balls he saw on the 12th hole of the Masters

"It's good sportsmanship to not pick up lost golf balls while they are still rolling."
Mark Twain

"Why the hell would people love that? I don't know. So Lee Trevino can make some more millions? It's a farce."

John McEnroe, on the Senior Tour

"You know how most golfers look. . . . They look in poor light like your brother-in-law. Plumbers have to be in better shape."

Jim Murray

"Too dull. It's a visual-neurological sport. It's so ridiculous."

Ralph Nader

"Golf remains, now as always, a sport geared toward fat men in plaid pants who think that *Fortune* magazine is racy."

Joe Queenan, columnist for various publications

"It may be popular, but it will never be cool."

Joe Queenan

GOLF CLUBS

"That yard-consuming club which more than any other has made a mockery of par."
Robert Trent Jones, on drivers

"When I hit iron, I say good-bye to ball."
Ayako Okamoto, on having problems with her irons

"I haven't even figured out what club I'm going to hit off the first tee."
Fuzzy Zoeller, asked what club he would give to Augusta to put on display if he won the Masters

GOLF WISDOM

"Golf is mostly a game of failures."
Tommy Armour

"This game is great and very strange."
Seve Ballesteros

"Other major American sports may be more consistently exciting, but no game has greater potential than golf for producing the cosmic gasp."
Tom Boswell

"Success is a choice; therefore, so is failure."
Bob Brue

"In golf as in life, the attempt to do something in one stroke that needs two is apt to result in taking three."
Walter Camp

"Golf is not a funeral, though both can be very sad affairs."
Bernard Darwin

"The best part is I've taken five strokes off my golf game."
Ellen DeGeneres, on coming out of the closet

"Golfers just love punishment. And that's where I come in."
Pete Dye, golf-course architect

"Golf can be a very depressing game if you're not careful, because players don't win every time."
Jim Ferree

"It's a game of adjustments, a game of constant change and adjustment."
Ben Hogan

"If you can't enjoy the time in between the golf shots, then you're going to have a very difficult life, because most of your life is the time spent in between."
Peter Jacobsen

"Golf professionals are like bears in the zoo. We may be fun to watch, but we aren't the game. The game is the millions of people that come out every day and play golf because they love it."
Peter Jacobsen

"Just tee it up and hit it, and when you find it, hit it again."
Don January, on his golfing philosophy

"Golf is like eating peanuts. You can play too much or too little."
Bobby Jones

"Golf is a game that creates emotions that sometimes cannot be sustained with the club still in one's hand."
Bobby Jones

"Golf is usually played with the outward appearance of great dignity. It is, nevertheless, a game of considerable passion—either of the explosive type or that which burns inwardly."
Bobby Jones

"You can discuss a tennis match in twenty minutes. But a golf round you go over hole by hole, strike by strike, and by the time four recaps are finished the sun is rising on a new day."
Alan King

"In golf, monotony is the spice of life."
Tom Kite

"Golf is nobody's game."
Willie Mays

"It's not a game. It's a hoodoo. A malevolent spirit. It hates real prowess. It punishes virtuosity. It has contempt for ability."

Jim Murray

"Life may not be fair, but golf is downright malicious."

Jim Murray

"Golf is a game of rhythm, style, grace, not brute strength. It is a meticulous game, best played by persons who are neat."

Jim Murray

"In golf, they say you're only as good as your last four-putt. It's like that in every sport—you've got to keep producing."

Terry Murray, NHL hockey coach

"It will slay you and mutilate you."

Mac O'Grady

"One minute you have total volition and willpower. Next minute, you can't tie your own shoelaces."

Mac O'Grady, on playing a round of golf that featured four birdies and three bogies

"One second you're on top of the world and the next you're struggling like baby turtles coming off the Galápagos Islands."

Mac O'Grady

"Golf is the cruelest game, because eventually it will drag you out in front of the whole school, take your lunch money, and slap you around."

Rick Reilly, Sports Illustrated

"Golf is 20 percent mechanics and technique. The other 80 percent is philosophy, humor, tragedy, romance, melodrama, companionship, camaraderie, cussedness, and conversation."

Grantland Rice

"Peeled down to his shorts, a highball in one hand and an attested scorecard in the other, it's hard for a man to be anything but himself."

Grantland Rice

"Golf is a funny game. One day you think you're the best in the world and the next you feel like nothing."

Chi Chi Rodriguez

"Most of us are perfectionists in a game where you can't obtain perfection."

Scott Simpson

"Keep close count of your nickels and dimes, stay away from whiskey, and never concede a putt."

Sam Snead

"I tried. I swung. I missed. I never tried again."

Aleksandr Solzhenitsyn, Soviet writer and dissident, on golf

"Golf isn't a game, it's a curse. It wasn't created by the shepherds of St. Andrews but by the witches from *Macbeth*."

Art Spander, columnist

"Golf is an all-demanding endeavor that has no beginning and no end. It can devour a man with its insatiable appetite."

Peter Thomson

"All a guy needs to keep going in tournament golf is good health, the same ambition he had when he was younger, and maybe two or three putts that fall at the right time."

Lee Trevino

"Golf, like measles, should be caught young."

P. G. Wodehouse

"Real golf is a thing of the spirit, not of mere mechanical excellence of stroke."

P. G. Wodehouse

"To find a man's true character, play golf with him."

P. G. Wodehouse

"The old trite saying of 'one shot at a time'? It wasn't trite to me. I lived it."

Mickey Wright

"I play the game the way it gives me pleasure. If I've got a 50-50 chance to pull off a shot, I say, 'Hell, let's go for it.'"

Fuzzy Zoeller

"Golf is not a fair game. It's a rude game."
Fuzzy Zoeller

GONE FISHIN'

"I feel great. I made enough money to go fishing."
*JoAnne Carner, on finishing second at
the Dinah Shore Classic, two days
before her 50th birthday*

"I might. I might also be forty miles offshore,
fishing."
*Curtis Strange, asked if he would
watch the U.S. Open playoff after
missing a chance to capture his third
U.S. Open in a row*

GRAND SLAMS

"From now on, he's going to have trouble even breathing."

> *Arnold Palmer, on the pressure Jack Nicklaus would feel after winning the first half of the Grand Slam (the Masters and the U.S. Open)*

"The impregnable quadrilateral of golf."
> *George Trevor, on the four majors*

GRASS IS
ALWAYS GREENER

"Grass . . . especially deep rough."
> *Ben Crenshaw, asked if he had any allergies*

"There are not enough weeds on this course to be like a European course."

> *Sandy Lyle, comparing Augusta to European courses*

"Next year, wear something that doesn't clash with green."

Jack Nicklaus, on giving the Masters green jacket to Larry Mize after Nicklaus won it the previous year

"If the one they have is too big, I can wait for the alterations."

Corey Pavin, on dreaming of winning the Masters and having a suit size of 37

"I wonder what size Craig Stadler's was in 1982. It must have looked like a nightgown."

Corey Pavin, on Craig Stadler's green jacket

"Isn't that the damnedest thing? It just hangs in my cupboard. I've never worn it anyplace except my house."

Gary Player, on his green jacket

"I think I'd look great. It's the same color as money."

> *Lee Trevino, on how he would look in a Masters suit*

"Green and black go well together."

> *Earl Woods, on Tiger Woods winning the '97 Masters and putting on the green jacket*

"I slept with it last night."

> *Tiger Woods, the day after winning the Masters, on the green jacket*

"It's mine now."

> *Ian Woosnam, who's 5'4", after scrambling to find a green jacket that would fit him and being asked whose it was*

"I really need to win to get another green jacket, because the one I have doesn't fit. I've gotten a bit fat."

> *Ian Woosnam, asked what motivated him to win the Masters five years after his '91 victory*

GREENS

"It's tough to read dirt."

> *Tommy Bolt, on unimpressive putting*
> *surfaces at a tournament*

"I put down a dime to mark my ball and it slid all the way off the green."

> *Gay Brewer, on the fast greens on a*
> *course in Ohio*

"It's a beautiful course, but the greens were so fast you had a better chance on I-209 [a freeway]."

> *Ken Green, on Augusta*

"Greens never bother me as long as they have a hole in them."

> *Simon Hobday, on players*
> *complaining about greens*

"They're so fast you have to figure out how to stop a ball before you hit it."

> *Jack Nicklaus, on fast greens at the*
> *1971 U.S. Open at Merion*

GURUS

"They're parasites living off the carcass of the sport. I'm not one of those sleazy people."

> *Mac O'Grady, on being characterized as a golf guru*

WALTER HAGEN

"The difference, as there is so often between Hagen and the other man, is that Hagen just won and the other man just did not."

> *Bernard Darwin*

"If I happen to start out with four 5s, I simply figure that I've used up my quota. I forget them and start out on a new track."

> *Walter Hagen, on his philosophy of getting four 5s during a match*

"If it were not for you, Walter, this dinner tonight would be downstairs in the pro shop and not in the ballroom."

> *Arnold Palmer, at a tribute to Hagen*

"Ben Hogan for President. If we're going to have a golfer, let's have a good one."

> *Anonymous, slogan during the 1956 presidential campaign directed against incumbent president Eisenhower, who spent a great deal of time golfing*

"Eisenhower isn't a Communist. He's a golfer."

> *Russell Baker, New York Times columnist, to a conservative who accused President Eisenhower of being a Communist*

"It's golf, golf, golf—interspersed with politics."

> *Senator John Breaux, describing a recent agenda of President Clinton*

"As if we don't have enough violence on television."

> *Barbara Bush, after watching her husband and Presidents Clinton and Ford on the golf course at the Bob Hope Classic*

"If Bill Clinton is an 8-handicap, I'm Bobby Jones."

> *George Bush, on Clinton's claim of being an 8-handicap*

"Greg Norman."

> *President Clinton, response to those who claimed he had a large lead in the polls over Bob Dole, a reference to Greg Norman's huge lead in a Masters tournament Norman lost on the last day to Nick Faldo*

"I was hot. I was smoking 'em. Even a blind pig finds an acorn sometimes."

> *President Clinton, on shooting his first 79*

"The best perk of this office is who you get to play golf with. I've played with Jack Nicklaus, Arnold Palmer, Raymond Floyd, Amy Alcott."

> *President Clinton*

"I've got a new idea. Try the fairway."

> *President Clinton, said to one of his foursome who hit a bad shot*

"There ought to be a law against asking a golfer what he shot."

President Dwight Eisenhower

"I may not know enough about being president, but I do know that a lot of decisions can be made on the golf course."

President Warren Harding

"Forget that I am president of the United States. I am Warren Harding, playing with some friends, and I'm going to beat the hell out of them."

President Harding

"Don't ever walk in front of them."

Scott Hoch, on what he learned from playing golf with Presidents Bush, Clinton, and Ford

"He plays such a great game of golf for a guy wearing skis."

Bob Hope, on President Gerald Ford

"He has a special kind of people in his gallery—the ones who like to skydive and walk on hot coals."

Bob Hope, on the golf game of
Gerald Ford

"The Secret Service is in front of you. And the Air Force is flying over you. But the worst part is that the Marines are digging sand traps for your balls."

Bob Hope, on playing golf
with presidents

"Hit till you're happy."

President Lyndon Johnson, on his
golf strategy

"Congress."

President Johnson, asked his
handicap when he showed up at
the Masters

"Golf isn't like politics when Clinton can get to the center just by throwing Hillary over the side. Golf takes work."

Tony Kornheiser, Washington Post
columnist

"Absolutely not. I would have let him fall on his face."

Andrew Magee, asked if he would have caught President Clinton if he had fallen at Magee's house instead of Greg Norman's

"The greatest thrill of my life—even better than getting elected."

President Richard Nixon, on his first hole in one

"That's news to me. I'm a Republican anyway."

Greg Norman, on how he felt about President Clinton bringing his name up when talking about the possibility of losing to Bob Dole despite a big lead in the polls

"Golf is fine relief from the tensions of office, but we are getting a little tired of holding the bag."

Adlai Stevenson, on President Eisenhower's love of golf

"It should be indulged in when the opportunity arises, as every man who has played the game knows that it rejuvenates and stretches the span of life."

President William Howard Taft

"Golf is a game for people who are not active enough for baseball."

President Taft

HAIR IT IS (OR ISN'T)

"I call him Nudie because he ain't got no hair on his head."

Tommy Bolt, on Sam Snead

"Hidden under that famous straw hat of his is a slick spot as wide as some fairways I've seen."

Tommy Bolt, on Snead

"All those who turn in 36-hole scores will make the cut."

> *Rafael Alarcon, touring pro, on*
> *terrible conditions in the first round*
> *of the '86 Masters*

"They don't call it the Indianapolis 25. It's the 500."

> *John Cook, on being one stroke back*
> *halfway through the '87 Masters*

HALL OF FAME

"My headstone will read, 'Here lies Amy Alcott, winner of 29 tour titles, but not a member of the Hall of Fame.'"

> *Amy Alcott, on the rule of having to*
> *win 30 tournaments to qualify for the*
> *LPGA Hall of Fame*

"You need 30 wins to qualify for the Hall of Fame. It's important to me. Besides, it makes a good obituary."

> *JoAnne Carner, on winning her*
> *30th tournament*

"No other person is involved in your getting in there. And if you get there, it's great."

> *Kathy Whitworth, defending the*
> *LPGA Hall of Fame 30-win policy*

"If you're going to do that, let's don't call it the Hall of Fame, let's call it the Make Everybody Happy Club."

> *Mickey Wright, on a movement to*
> *lower standards for entry into the*
> *LPGA Hall of Fame*

HANDICAPS

"Drink and debauchery."

> *Lord Castlerosse, asked his handicap*

"Drinking on the golf course."

> *Bill Murray, asked his handicap*

"If you gave him a handicap he wanted, he'd beat your head in."

> *Gene Sarazen, on playing golf with*
> *Howard Hughes*

HAZELTINE (MINNESOTA)

"Some 80 acres of corn and a few cows."

> *Dave Hill, on the 1970 U.S. Open*
> *at Hazeltine*

"It wasn't a course, it was a firing squad."

> *Jim Murray*

"I frequently felt lost. I thought then that many players will need guides as well as caddies in this Open."

> *Jack Nicklaus, on the 1970*
> *U.S. Open*

HEIGHT REPORT

"I'm so small. I got my start in golf as a ball marker."
Chi Chi Rodriguez

"I eat soup off his head."
Jeff Sluman, 5'7", on 5'6" golfer Brian Kamm

HEY, MULLIGAN MAN

"Life's ultimate mulligan."
Dave Marr, describing the Senior Tour

"Can I have a mulligan?"
Chi Chi Rodriguez, after driving a shot into the rough on the first hole of the 1964 U.S. Open

SIMON HOBDAY

"It never ceases to amaze me how well he can hit a shot when he has the wrong club in his hand."
Paul Blanks, Hobday's caddie

BEN HOGAN

"On iron shots, he's so far ahead of anyone else that I don't even know who rates as second."
Frank Beard, on Ben Hogan being the best iron shooter even at age 53

"I've seen a lot of pros drop their clubs to go over to watch Ben Hogan practice. But I never saw Hogan drop his clubs to watch them practice."
Tommy Bolt

"Only way you beat Ben is if God wanted you to."
Tommy Bolt

"When you played with Hogan, he made you feel like you were holding your clubs upside down."
Bill Collins, former golf pro

"He was a cold, detached artisan on the course, likened by some observers to an undertaker wearing a shroud of defeat for his adversaries."
Will Grimsley, on Ben Hogan

"I don't like the glamour. I just like the game."
Ben Hogan

"Thank you. How did you do?"
Ben Hogan, said to Clayton Heafner, who finished second at the U.S. 1951 Open, two strokes behind Hogan

"His control of the ball was such that he seemed to allow it no option but to go where he wanted it to go."
Al Laney

"That little man is the only one in golf I've ever been afraid of."
Lloyd Mangrum

"He was the most dedicated practitioner of all time. His tenacity had no equal."

Paul Runyan

"He plays with the frigidity of dry ice. He is the most merciless of all the modern golfers."

Gene Sarazen

HOLE IN ONE

"Too much tax."

Isao Aoki, on not taking advantage of a condo he won in the United States for shooting a hole in one

"I rarely aimed at the flag. I aimed at the spot where I had the best birdie opportunity."

Ben Hogan, on his four career holes in one

"The perfect game of golf has never been played. It's 18 holes in one."

Ben Hogan, asked if he ever played a perfect game of golf

"A hole in one is amazing when you think of the different universes this white mass of molecules has to pass through on its way to the hole."
Mac O'Grady

"I don't remember it [the second] as much. I was still giddy from the first one."
Rick Ostidek, amateur golfer, on two consecutive holes in one at a Nebraska golf course

"It's my seventh, but I've never won a car."
Costantino Rocca, after shooting a hole in one at the Ryder Cup

"With the hole in one, it's very difficult to lose the hole."
Costantino Rocca, on the biggest advantage of his Ryder Cup hole in one

HOOK SHOT

"Drive fairways all the time, no fun. Make big hook, cause excitement."
Seve Ballesteros

HOOPS

"Golf is a scary game. The ball is too small."
Kareem Abdul-Jabbar

"Twenty-five years ago when you looked at the NBA, it was a bunch of skinny guys in bad shorts. Now it's muscular guys in bad shorts. It's the same thing in golf."
David Feherty, on the athleticism of current golfers

"They told me I had time to work on my game here. I didn't know they meant my golf game."
Steve Kerr, on averaging less than ten minutes a game after being acquired by the Orlando Magic

"I look at a golf course and see a great waste of pastureland."

> *Karl Malone, on being a*
> *cattle rancher*

"When I was growing up, my mother wouldn't allow me near a golf course. She didn't think the people were very nice. Now I play every day, and you know what? She was right."

> *Bill Russell*

"The tickets to the Bulls games—that's the best part."

> *Tiger Woods, on the best thing*
> *about being famous*

"Get involved with a sport like golf or tennis, sports that you can use for many years. Basketball is one of the first ones to desert you because of age."

> *George Yardley, Basketball Hall*
> *of Famer*

BOB HOPE

"This is the only event in the world where guys can get money out of the desert without drilling for oil."

> *Bob Hope, on his tournament*

"That one must have been hit by your brother, No Hope."

> *Tom Watson, on a bad shot by Bob Hope*

HORSE SENSE

"The first couple of rounds are like a mile-and-a-half horse race. You are jockeying for position."

> *Ray Floyd, on the first two rounds of the U.S. Open*

"I want to come back as Cigar. I think he's got it made."

> *Gary Player, asked who he would like to be if he were reincarnated*

"Shoemaker wasn't carrying the horse, the horse was carrying him. I've never seen a jockey carry the damn horse over the finish line."

>*Lee Trevino, on people comparing the accomplishment of Jack Nicklaus winning the Masters at age 46 with Willie Shoemaker winning the Kentucky Derby at age 53*

INJURY LIST

"It is like if I smack you in the face four times a day, you do not like it very much. But if I smack you only once a day, then you say, 'Hey, this feels good.'"

>*Jose-Maria Olazabal, on the lessening pain he felt after a foot injury*

INTELLIGENCE

"The greens are as small as my brain."

>*Hubert Green, on Inverness, home of the 1986 PGA*

"We all have stupid genes in us, and golf brings out the stupid genes."
John Madden

"You really don't get into deep conversations about the world. Most of the time you're talking about the bad bounce on number 7."
Gary McCord, on conversations during golf matches

"You always think you're getting smarter at this game, but every now and then you have a relapse and realize you're not as smart as you thought you were."
Arnold Palmer

"When the last shot of the Masters disappeared, a million thoughts went through my mind, what little mind I have."
Fuzzy Zoeller, after winning the '79 Masters

"He happened to play the great game with more magic and more grace than anyone before or since."

Alistair Cooke, on Jones

"His force as a golfer is transcended by his inestimable qualities as a human being."

President Dwight Eisenhower, on Jones

"Just walking around watching a match, he's still the biggest attraction in golf."

Ben Hogan

"While we were doing Peachtree I realized that there could be only one Bobby Jones, so I became Trent."

Robert Trent Jones, on designing the Peachtree golf course with Bobby Jones

"He has more character than any champion in our history."

O. B. Keeler

"When one had talked with him for a short time, he gave you the feeling that the only difference between your golf and his was that he had been much more lucky."

> *Raymond Oppenheimer, businessman*
> *who had the honor of playing golf*
> *with Jones*

"Golf seemed to have been invented just for him to come along and show us how well it could be played."

> *Charles Price*

"One might as well attempt to describe the smoothness of the wind as to paint a clear picture of his complete swing."

> *Grantland Rice*

"That rare sort of hero—in sports of any field—a man whose actual stature exceeds that of the mythological figure he has been made into."

> *Herbert Warren Wind*

TRENT JONES

"Saw a course you'd really like. On the first tee, you drop the ball off your left shoulder."

Jimmy Demaret, to legendary architect Robert Trent Jones

TOM KITE

"The two-legged Alydar."

Mike Downey, on Tom Kite's propensity for finishing second

"Tom is the rarest kind of genius. He has the ability to do the same thing every day all day long."

Johnny Miller, on the methodical brilliance of Kite

"I always thought if we put Langer on in the first match of the morning, we would all probably miss lunch."

> *Seve Ballesteros, on Langer's*
> *reputation for slow play*

"When has Langer ever been fined by the European tour? Never. Say no more."

> *Nick Price, complaining about the*
> *slow play of Langer*

"Bernhard's got a beard. He was clean shaven when we teed off."

> *Lee Trevino, on the slow-playing*
> *Langer sporting a two-day growth*

LEFTY

"It doesn't make a difference which side you
swing from. It just matters how soon you get it
in the hole."

Sam Adams, on being a lefty golfer

TOM LEHMAN

"People are really for him. I just like the guy
so much."

President Bill Clinton, on the
well-liked Lehman

"It took me 15 holes to think of a clean joke to
tell him."

Justin Leonard, on being paired with
straight-laced Tom Lehman

LIGHTNING
STRIKING AGAIN

"I felt like I was 6 feet 2, I got stretched out so far."

> *Lee Trevino, after being hit*
> *by lightning*

"When God wants to play through, you let him play through."

> *Lee Trevino, on being struck*
> *by lightning*

"What good is a posthumous entry to the U.S. Open?"

> *Greg Turner, European PGA player,*
> *on stopping play at the Volvo Masters*
> *in Spain during a lightning storm,*
> *when playing well would have*
> *qualified him for the U.S. Open*

GENE LITTLER

"No one can remember his last three-putt. He could par Mount Everest."

> *Jim Murray, on Gene Littler's consistency*

NANCY LOPEZ

"Nancy just proves that golf is easy. Her father fixed fenders in the morning and taught her to play in the afternoon."

> *Herb Graffis*

"I spent the whole day worrying about whether someone would see my underwear."

> *Nancy Lopez, on finishing second to Hollis Stacy in the '77 U.S. Women's Open after blaming her loss on a broken zipper*

"They say they've taken up a collection to send me on a three-week vacation."

> *Nancy Lopez, on how the touring*
> *pros have responded to her amazing*
> *success as a rookie at age 21*

"She plays by feel. All her senses come into play. That's when golf is an art."

> *Carol Mann, on Lopez*

LOSING

"Gary's the guy who played good enough to win it. I'm the guy who played just good enough to blow it."

> *Hubert Green, on Gary Player*
> *beating Green and several others by*
> *one stroke at the '78 Masters*

"To lose a game is not a national calamity. This will act as a tonic all around."

> *Walter Hagen, after the United States*
> *lost the Ryder Cup*

"I'm known as the scarecrow in the American circuit. Scare them I do, beat them I don't."

> *Howie Johnson, touring golf pro who was close to the lead in the first round of the '71 British Open*

"When you feel a fool, and a bad golfer to boot, what can you do except to throw the club away?"

> *Bobby Jones*

"It was fun watching the other three guys play."

> *Justin Leonard, on the PGA Slam Finals, in which Leonard was six strokes back of third place and only four players competed*

"I know I screwed up today, but it's not the end of the world for me. I've got forty million bucks."

> *Greg Norman, after his collapse in the final round of the '96 Masters*

"You get the taste of success, you see the filet mignon and reach for the Rothschild wine, and then you see that it's Gallo."

> *Mac O'Grady*

"Throwing up on myself."

> *Curtis Strange, on what he felt like*
> *doing after losing the 1985 Masters*

LOVE LIFE

"Ever since my wife found it in the glove compartment."

> *Lee Trevino, asked when he started*
> *wearing a corset for his bad back*

"This year was the first time I've ever been engaged and dating at the same time."

> *Tiger Woods, on all the gossip*
> *about him*

LUCK BE A LADY

"First you've got to be good, but then you've got to be lucky."

> *Harry Cooper*

"When you work very hard, you get lucky. And when they say you're lucky, that's when you know you have arrived."

Chi Chi Rodriguez

SANDY LYLE

"I'm glad he's going home. I can't wait to get rid of the guy. Who knows how many tournaments he'd win if he stayed here all year?"

Mark Calcavecchia, upon hearing that Lyle was heading back to Europe

"My girlfriend tickles my feet at night, and that clears my nose."

Sandy Lyle, asked how he recovered from a cold during the Masters

"Just think, if it hadn't been for Paul Revere, all this would belong to you."

Lee Trevino, upon teeing up at the Masters with Sandy Lyle, who is English

"I certainly don't get the same feeling when I tee it up here on Thursday as I do when I tee it up at Augusta National."

> *Mark Calcavecchia, asked if he considered the Players Championship a major*

"The majors are what golf's all about. The other ones you play for the prize money. These you play to get your name on a piece of silver."

> *Nick Faldo*

"In other sports they don't do anything differently than they have done all year, but golf is the only game that changes for a major event."

> *Ray Floyd*

"I think a career is complete when you finish it."

> *Tom Kite, asked if he thought his career would be complete should he win one of the majors*

"I think Darth Vader is actually a USGA official."

Johnny Miller, on the course preparations for major championships

"Maybe if I knock on the door enough, the door will open one day."

Colin Montgomerie, on coming close to winning a major

"They talk about the majors and how important they are. But you're playing the same guys you play every week, just on another golf course."

Sam Snead

"Were you in prison in 1984? Maybe you didn't get copies of the newspaper there?"

Lee Trevino, 1984 PGA winner, upon being told by a reporter during the '86 U.S. Open that he hadn't won a major in a long time

"This is truly the national championship of U.S. golf."

> *Steve Melnyk, on the U.S. Open*

"Darkness is fading."

> *Steve Melnyk*

"I used my t'ree iron."

> *Arnold Palmer, explaining in a Brooklyn accent what club he used when he had to climb a tree in an Australian tournament*

"Of all the rounds I've played, this is definitely one of them."

> *Paul Stankowski*

"You could play cards and you're waiting for the card you need, and there's a lot of stress for a big pot. That didn't help him any."

> *Sam Snead, on why the talented Mangrum did not win more tournaments*

MARRIAGE

"My wife, Barbara, followed me around all day. Now she knows better."

> *Jack Nicklaus, on playing the U.S. Open at Winged Foot, 24 years after he played there during his honeymoon*

"I have known cases where marriage has improved a man's game and other cases where it seemed to put him right off stroke."

> *P. G. Wodehouse*

"Happiness is a husband and a wife with practically identical handicaps."
P. G. Wodehouse

MASTERS

"Just like going to the moon . . . it's unbelievable."
*George Archer, on winning
the Masters*

"He could be the first player to ever win the Masters who doesn't shave."
Paul Azinger, on Tiger Woods

"I love it when I get here and I hate it when I leave."
Paul Azinger, on Augusta

"It isn't just a stop on the American tour. It's a shrine with a par of 72."
Furman Bisher, on the Masters

"It's like taking the first step on a high wire across Niagara Falls."

Jackie Burke, on the first hole at the Masters

"Never."

Billy Casper, on when someone would break Jack Nicklaus's course record of 271 in the '65 Masters (broken by Tiger Woods in '97)

"They [the top names] shouldn't mind letting us poor boys have something now and then."

Charlie Coody, on winning the '71 Masters

"It's just a road with pavement, like some of the roads back in Dardanelle [Arkansas]."

John Daly, on Magnolia Lane

"You've built a bridge for Nelson and a bridge for Hogan and you've put up a plaque for Sarazen. I've won the Masters three times. Don't you think you might put my name on one of those little green outhouses?"

Jimmy Demaret, to Cliff Roberts, Masters chairman

"You need a touch like Houdini's at Augusta, but in the end you always have fond memories of the place. That's why you play."
Doug Ford

"You win all the Tucsons, all the Kemps, all the Iron City Opens—you can, nobody remembers. You win a Masters, nobody ever forgets."
Bob Goalby

"Just a road with some trees on it."
Ken Green, on Magnolia Lane

"We don't want to become the Pizza Hut Masters."
Hord Hardin, Masters chairman, on refusing to get involved with sponsors

"This is the only course I know where you choke when you come in the gate."
Lionel Hebert, on Augusta

"They'll probably find him hanging from a tree on number 7."
Dave Hill, on Rod Curl shooting a 6 on the par-3 6th hole of the Masters

"If the Masters offered no money at all, I would be here trying just as hard."

Ben Hogan

"Tiger Woods on Sunday at the '97 Masters was the biggest lock in sports since Secretariat at the Belmont."

Dan Jenkins, on Tiger Woods

"When the golf course is wet and the wind quiet, it is easy. We always hope it will not be that way during the first week of April."

Bobby Jones

"There isn't a single hole that can't be birdied if you just think. But there isn't one that can't be double bogeyed if you ever stop thinking."

Bobby Jones

"I'll be back every year if I have to walk 1,500 miles to do it."

Herman Keiser, winner of the '46 Masters

"I won my tournament. I won the silver medal."

> *Tom Kite, on finishing second at the '97 Masters, 12 shots behind Tiger Woods*

"Yeah, take a 12."

> *Dave Marr, after his friend Arnold Palmer, who had a six-shot lead entering the final hole of the '64 Masters, asked Marr if there was anything he could do to help him in his fight for second place*

"It's amazing that they took Bobby Jones's little fun event and turned it into an event that may be more important than our national championship."

> *Johnny Miller*

"They have nothing like this place back home in Europe. For them, the Masters must be like going on a blind date, opening the door, and being greeted by Sharon Stone."

> *Johnny Miller, on foreign players at the Masters*

"I think my only thought was, 'Oh my goodness, oh my goodness, oh my goodness.'"

> *Larry Mize, on hitting a 140-foot*
> *shot at the 11th green en route to*
> *winning the 1987 Masters*

"The whole day was a highlight for me, so let's start with breakfast, shall we?"

> *Colin Montgomerie, asked to recap*
> *the day after shooting a second-round*
> *67 at the Masters*

"With Nicklaus winning the Masters, God's in his heaven and all's right with the world."

> *Jim Murray, on Jack Nicklaus*
> *winning the Masters at age 46*

"In Japan, when spring comes, people think about the Masters."

> *Tommy Nakajima*

"He went from 'Houston we have a problem,' to, 'Huston, we have a leader.'"

> *Jim Nantz, on John Huston becoming*
> *the first-round leader of the '97*
> *Masters because of an eagle on the*
> *18th hole*

"I sort of welled up four or five times coming in."
Jack Nicklaus, on winning the '86
Masters at age 46

"I don't think about winning the Masters as part of the Slam. You want to win the Masters because of what it means to the game."
Jack Nicklaus

"This is where God hangs out."
Mac O'Grady, on the Masters

"It's like a mountain climber going to Mount Everest. He's climbed Mount McKinley and he's climbed the Andes in Chile, but he doesn't know what Mount Everest is like until he gets there."
Mac O'Grady, on the Masters

"Today, I felt as if I was playing a game of checkers. It was easy. Yesterday, I felt as if I was playing a game of chess with Bobby Fischer. I didn't have a chance."
Mac O'Grady, on shooting a
first-round 82 and a second-round
70 at the Masters

"I thought 6s were for other people."

Arnold Palmer, on shooting a 6 on
the 18th hole of the Masters

"Cut down by Amen Corner, but we gave 'em a few thrills, didn't we?"

Billy Joe Patton, who led the 1954
Masters on Saturday but shot a 7 on
the 13th hole in the final round

"Every shot here is within a fraction of disaster—that's what makes it so great."

Gary Player

"I don't know of any similarities between this golf course and anything on the planet."

Mike Reid, asked to compare
Augusta with other courses

"Maybe if I only have to play nine holes."

Costantino Rocca, on the possibility
of catching Tiger Woods after being
nine shots back going into the last
round of the '97 Masters

"I'm the last guy you expected to see."

> *Lee Trevino, upon walking into the*
> *interview room with the first-round*
> *lead in the '89 Masters*

"It's not one of my favorite places. My car even goes off the road there."

> *Lee Trevino, on the Masters*

"If the Masters had a rough, we wouldn't finish in two weeks."

> *Lee Trevino*

"If justice were poetic, Hubert Green would win every year."

> *John Updike, on all the green that*
> *surrounds the Masters*

"This is an event, not a tournament. This is just like the Kentucky Derby."

> *Tom Watson, on how he felt about*
> *advertising at the Masters*

"The margin of error and element of luck are more relevant at Augusta than anyplace I've seen."

> *Tom Weiskopf*

"Leave all the social significance aside. This is like watching Babe Ruth in the 1920s."

George Will, on Tiger Woods winning the '97 Masters

"The greatest natural laxative in the world."

Fuzzy Zoeller, on the first hole of the Masters

"If that's golf, I'm in the wrong damn league."

Fuzzy Zoeller, complaining about the conditions of the greens at the Masters

"I'd like to thank Tom and Ed for missing all those putts."

Fuzzy Zoeller, after winning the '79 Masters due in part to some missed clutch putts by Tom Watson and Ed Sneed

"Because you pray after you play."

Fuzzy Zoeller, asked how Amen Corner got its name

"He may not be popular in the locker room, but he is in the living room."

> *Dick Ebersol, NBC Sports' president,*
> *on the controversial Johnny Miller,*
> *who is often critical of other players*

"Thanks from the heart of my bottom."

> *Nick Faldo, acknowledging the*
> *British press for making his divorce*
> *sound so scandalous*

"That's a recipe for disaster."

> *David Feherty, on being teamed with*
> *Gary McCord for an announcer*
> *tryout*

"He is not exactly the Edward R. Murrow of golf."

> *Frank Hannigan, U.S. Golf*
> *Association president, on*
> *Gary McCord*

"Sportswriters aren't very good golfers, so maybe it's rubbed off."

> *Roger Maltbie, on writing a guest*
> *column for the* San Francisco
> Chronicle *while having a bad round*
> *at the U.S. Open*

"Trumpy doesn't know a graphite shaft from an elevator shaft."

> *Mark Solatu,* San Francisco
> Chronicle, *on Bob Trumpy's*
> *announcing of the Ryder Cup*

"Being on television hasn't helped or hurt my game, but it's helped my bank account."
> *Lee Trevino*

"When I hear athletes not talking to the press, I think what fools they are."

> *Lee Trevino, on golfers losing out on*
> *endorsement money because they*
> *won't deal with the media*

"If we played a course like this every week, there wouldn't be anybody left at the end of the season. We'd all quit the game."

> *Mark Calcavecchia, on Medinah*

"They ought to dynamite that green. It looked like the guy that did it had a mask on. Had to be Jesse James."

> *Billy Casper, on the 16th hole at Medinah*

"The special mission of any Open is to make the golfers miserable, and Medinah will have no trouble doing that."

> *Bernie Lincicome, columnist,*
> Chicago Tribune

"Medinah has fangs."
> *Jim Murray*

"Medinah will ultimately win. It always has."
> *Jack Nicklaus, on lots of low scores early in the 1990 U.S. Open*

"This course is like fighting Mike Tyson. You get through and you're glad. You don't have the energy to get excited."
>
> *Tim Simpson*

"A great course. You hit a good shot and you get a reward. Hit a bad shot and you have to work your fanny off."
>
> *Fuzzy Zoeller*

MENTAL GAME

"To forget."
>
> *Seve Ballesteros, asked the secret of golf*

"The mind messes up more shots than the body."
>
> *Tommy Bolt*

"I'm not enthusiastic about a hot round or too depressed about a cold one. I decided that blowing my top would kill my chances of making it big in golf."
>
> *Tony Lema*

"You don't have to walk off the course like you've just been in the Great Crusades."

Roger Maltbie, on having fun in golf

"The same way you do."

Jack Nicklaus, asked how he missed an 18-inch putt

"I love to watch Oprah, Geraldo, all the shows about dysfunctionals. That's my psychoanalysis."

Mac O'Grady

"Golf is a movement of joints coordinated by the cerebellum. It's as simple as that."

Mac O'Grady

"I just play."

Patty Sheehan, after Tom Kite asked her what technical aspects of her game she thought about during a tournament

"Thinking instead of acting is the number-one golf disease."

Sam Snead

"Golf is at least 50 percent a mental game, and if you recognize that the mind prompts us physically, you can almost say golf is entirely a mental effort."
Peter Thomson

"There's no competitor I don't fear. But I use fear to my advantage."
Lee Trevino

"I didn't realize how much confidence means in this game until I didn't have any."
Bob Tway

"We really have to play with 15 clubs. We have 14 in our bag and the 15th is our head."
Greg Twiggs, touring pro

"It's just like your grandmother. Beautiful, honored, getting on a little in years, and loving. But you do just one thing wrong and she'll whop you."

> *Charlie Crenshaw, Ben Crenshaw's*
> *father, on what he told Ben*
> *about Merion*

"Merion isn't great because history was written there. History was made there because Merion is great."

> *Pete Dye*

"The trouble with Merion is that it always has you on the defensive. There's no way you can take the offense on it."

> *Ben Hogan*

"There are a lot of birdie holes, but there are a lot that make you eat your lunch."

> *Johnny Miller*

"Putting the cream of U.S. golfers against this pitiable little piece of real estate was Notre Dame against Susquehanna."

Jim Murray

"I love Merion, and I don't even know her last name."

Lee Trevino, after winning the U.S. Open at Merion

PHIL MICKELSON

"I've never been to a Ryder Cup, but that must be what it's like for the foreign team."

Justin Leonard, on all the fans cheering for Phil Mickelson at Phoenix

MILITARY WATCH

"Because they wanted to put me where I could do the least damage."

> *Hubert Green, on why he was a cook in the National Guard*

"The golf course is your enemy, and when you go to war, you've got to defeat the enemy. It's 18 individual battles, and a golf course takes no prisoners."

> *Earl Woods*

JOHNNY MILLER

"To shoot like that in the final round of the U.S. Open, well, that was doggone near superhuman."

> *Billy Casper, on Johnny Miller shooting a last-round 63 to win the 1973 U.S. Open*

"I'd like to have that boy's nerve in this tired old body."

> *Sam Snead, on Miller*

"Larry Mize was the best thing to come out of the South since Kentucky Fried Chicken."

>*Mike Raper, British oddsmaker, on bookmakers making a lot of money at the '87 Masters because few people bet on the winner—Larry Mize*

MONEY MAKES THE WORLD GO 'ROUND

"You finally make enough money to buy these things and now they end up giving them to you."

>*Paul Azinger, on getting all kinds of free shoes and shirts after winning the Phoenix Open*

"We had a small wager, but the outcome did not affect the Forbes rating."

>*Warren Buffett, on playing golf with Bill Gates*

"I don't care if you're the tiddledywinks champ, because in America that's how we do business. Money is how we keep score."

> *Jim Colbert, on criticism that the seniors make too much money*

"I'm working on my second million. I completely gave up on my first million."

> *Lou Graham, asked if he made a million after winning the U.S. Open in '75*

"When I started out [in 1968], I didn't think $200,000 was attainable. To add another zero, and it is mind-boggling."

> *Hale Irwin, on the money he has won during his illustrious career*

"At first, I said, 'Let's play for taxes.'"

> *Michael Jordan, on playing golf with President Clinton*

"The boys on Wall Street better get up early tomorrow morning."

> *Wayne Levi, a stock market investor, after winning $180,000 at the Central Western Open*

"The money is completely unimportant—once you have won enough of it."

Johnny Miller

"In the old days, the goal was to become the head pro of a nice club. Now the idea is to buy the club."

Chi Chi Rodriguez

"I'm not going to the cemetery broke."

Gene Sarazen, asked at age 95 if the current players' huge winnings bothered him

"It's important to just play the golf tour and become really wealthy. On tour, Uncle Sam's your partner. He sits there in Washington, watching on the tube and seeing exactly how much you earn."

Lee Trevino

"The world's a funny place. When you have no money, no one will do anything for you. If you become successful and pile up enough money to buy anything you want, people deluge you with gifts you don't need and try to do all kinds of things for you."

Lee Trevino

"To win enough tournaments to put my caddie among the top 20 money winners."

Lee Trevino, on his ambitions

"I hope they [bookmakers] lost a lot of money. It was an insult to make me one of the outsiders at 11 to 1."

Ian Woosnam, after winning the World Match Play tournament in 1987

"I tip more than that at bars."

Fuzzy Zoeller, on his first-year earnings of $7,000

MONSTER MASH

"Every golfer has a little monster in him. It's just that type of sport."

Fuzzy Zoeller

COLIN MONTGOMERIE

"A warthog who's just been stung by a wasp."
*David Feherty, describing one of
Montgomerie's facial expressions*

"He's a few french fries short of a Happy Meal."
*David Feherty, on some of the
outlandish comments of Montgomerie*

ORVILLE MOODY

"They all came, they all played, this man won, and
that's it."

*Henry Longhurst, on critics
complaining about Orville Moody's
victory at the 1969 U.S. Open*

MUIRFIELD VILLAGE
(Ohio)

"Such immaculate conditions that people would sooner have dropped cigarette butts on their babies' tummies."

> *Dan Jenkins, on the conditions at*
> *Muirfield Village*

"Like standing on the street corner and burning $100 bills."

> *Mark McCormack, superagent,*
> *on his early misgivings about*
> *Jack Nicklaus's creation of*
> *Muirfield Village*

MUSIC TO MY EARS

"I'm a rhythm picker, man, who spent ten years tryin' to be an overnight success. Now here I am with Arnie and the fellas."

> *Glen Campbell, on the Glen*
> *Campbell L.A. Open*

"My golf game wasn't much, but then, have you heard Nicklaus and Palmer sing?"

Dean Martin

NAP TIME

"I fall asleep on the course. Just look at my scores."

Gay Brewer, at age 62, asked how he can combine his naps with his golf game

"The only thing you do better as a senior than you did at 26 is sleep."

Dave Hill, Senior Tour player

"It looks like he had a $5 Nassau and lost his pants."

> *Robert Boyd, on playing partner*
> *Forest Fezler, who took off his pants*
> *and wore shorts—the first time that*
> *happened in the 83-year history of*
> *the U.S. Open*

"I just loaned Bolivia $2 million, but I play $1 Nassaus."

> *President Dwight Eisenhower*

"You start playing for big dollars and you're a clown and crazy like I am, you're going to get a 2-iron between your eyes."

> *Lee Trevino*

BYRON NELSON

"He plays golf shots like a virtuoso."

> *Tommy Armour, on Byron Nelson*

"I want you all to know that I played golf with that man last year and outdrove him twice."

President Dwight Eisenhower, pointing out Byron Nelson to a group of dignitaries

"People thought I was boring. I used to just hit it on the fairway, on the green, then hole the putt."

Byron Nelson

"Byron didn't drink, smoke, gamble, or chase women. I don't think he had any fun out there."

Sam Snead, at a roast for Nelson

"Never mind 11 in a row. You can't win 11 in a year if you traveled all over the world and counted the Uganda and Beirut Open."

Lee Trevino, on the amazing 11-tournament-in-a-row winning streak of Byron Nelson

"Nelson chews you up and spits you out. How can anyone beat him?"

Mike Turnesa, on Byron Nelson

"A baby-faced chicken killer."

> *Dave Marr, on Larry Nelson's quiet*
> *demeanor and killer instinct*

NOISE

"What train?"

> *Ben Hogan, asked if a loud train*
> *nearby bothered him during a key*
> *shot at the U.S. Open*

"The best thing is a space helmet like [those at]
NASA. You put it on, it blocks out things on
both sides."

> *Mac O'Grady, on methods to avoid*
> *being disturbed on the golf course*

NUMBERS GAME

"There are no birdies or bogeys, no eagles or double bogeys; there are only numbers. If you can get this way, you can play this game."
Jim Colbert

"You've just joined the Bo Derek club."
Wayne Grady, who once shot two 10s within a month, to Arnold Palmer, who had just shot a 10 at the British Open

OAKLAND HILLS
(MICHIGAN)

"The Monster [Oakland Hills] bit back."
Dave Barr, on Andy North winning the '85 U.S. Open with a final-round 74

"My first wife was nicer than this course."
John Daly, on Oakland Hills

"The greatest test of golf I have ever played, and the toughest course."
Ben Hogan

"They just didn't give you any room to shoot. You had to be almost perfect with every shot, and nobody can really make every shot."
Ben Hogan

"The player with the best shots, swing, and nerve control has the best chance to win."
Robert Trent Jones

"You have to walk down there single file."
Dr. Cary Middlecoff, on thin fairways at Oakland Hills

"Yesterday it was difficult. Today, it's difficult. Tomorrow, it will be difficult. . . . It hasn't changed in 35 years."
Jack Nicklaus

"I don't think people would build a golf course with greens like this these days. They would be ridiculed and asked not to build any more golf courses."

Payne Stewart

"If there's just a little bit of bitching, the course must be great."

Curtis Strange

"I'm just glad I'm not a member here, because I'd have to play here every day."

Curtis Strange

"This golf course is too hard, it's just too hard. . . . It's the type of golf course where you just don't make bogeys—you make double bogeys."

Jim Thorpe

OAKMONT (PENNSYLVANIA)

"The final degree in the college of golf."

Tommy Armour, on Oakmont

"I was buried in a trap so deep you could have thrown a little dirt and covered me up."
Tommy Bolt, on Oakmont

"I'm going to have to practice putting by trying to roll the ball down the drain in my bathtub."
Jim Gallagher, on the
Oakmont greens

"Putting here is like playing pool in the dark."
Gary Hallberg

"It is certain that nowhere is there a more brutal test."
Mark McCormack

"This is a course where good putters worry about their second putt before they hit the first one."
Lew Worsham, on the fast greens
of Oakmont

"You can't charge this course, you have to romance it a little bit."

> *Billy Casper, on Olympic*
> *Country Club*

"This is not an Open, it's a punishment for our sins. It's not a golf course, it's a penal colony."

> *Jim Murray, on holding the 1987*
> *U.S. Open at Olympic Country Club*

"Playing this course is like Russian roulette. One bad shot and it's all over."

> *Mac O'Grady*

"The inclinations and topography of Olympic Club already disturb the vesicular semicircular canals of my inner-ear balancing system."

> *Mac O'Grady*

"Always looks like the last guy to climb out of the clown car at the circus."

> *Dan Jenkins, on the*
> *eccentric Parnevik*

"It's really expensive. I don't know why. It tastes just like regular dirt."

> *Jesper Parnevik, on eating*
> *volcanic dust to clean his*
> *gastrointestinal system*

PARTY ON

"No, but I've sponsored several New York taverns."

> *Ray Floyd, asked if he was sponsored*
> *by a New York tavern when he*
> *turned pro*

"A fifth at night, a 68 in the morning."

> *Walter Hagen, describing an*
> *ideal day*

"Twice this month I had to get up at 7 A.M. Sometimes I'm coming in at that time."
>   Doug Sanders, complaining about the Senior Tour

"I had to be on the tee so early I did not even have time to throw up."
>   Doug Sanders, on playing at the British Open

"I would have to say his outstanding characteristic is his ability to have a good time."
>   Sue Stadler, on her husband Craig

COREY PAVIN

"He's like a little dog that gets ahold of your pants legs and won't let go."
>   Mark O'Meara, on the relentless Pavin

PEBBLE BEACH
(CALIFORNIA)

"The best 17-hole golf course in the world."
> *Jimmy Demaret, criticizing the*
> *18th hole at Cypress Point, a*
> *340-yard dogleg*

"Pebble Beach is Alcatraz with grass."
> *Bob Hope*

"A book of case histories could be written about Pebble's atrocities that would make Edgar Allan Poe read like Nancy Drew."
> *Dan Jenkins*

"It's supposed to be like a trip through Indian territory at night, a visit to a haunted house."
> *Jim Murray*

"The way I play hasn't diminished my enthusiasm for Pebble Beach, but it has diminished my enthusiasm for my game."
> *Jack Nicklaus, on not making the cut*
> *at the '92 U.S. Open at Pebble Beach*

"I just came here to play golf and got lucky."
*John Daly, on winning the 1991 PGA
tournament as a virtual unknown*

PGA WEST (CALIFORNIA)

"I know some courses which are easier than the practice greens here."
Lee Trevino, on PGA West

"After the tournament they ought to have a roll call, because I wouldn't be surprised if a couple of players have been down there for a couple of days."
*Lee Trevino, on PGA West, home of
the '95 Legends of Golf tournament*

PINE VALLEY
(NEW JERSEY)

"It is all very well to punish a bad stroke, but the right of eternal punishment should be reserved for a higher tribunal than a greens committee."

Bernard Darwin, on the difficult 8th hole at Pine Valley

"While playing Pine Valley can be a penance, and nearly always is somewhere during the round, the agonies are the price which must be paid for the ecstasies."

Peter Dobereiner, golf columnist

PINEHURST
(NORTH CAROLINA)

"The man who doesn't feel emotionally stirred when he golfs at Pinehurst should be ruled out of golf for life."

Tommy Armour, on Pinehurst

PLAYOFFS

"I like head-to-head, because I was a hustler all my life."

> *Lee Trevino, on winning the '71 U.S. Open playoff against Jack Nicklaus*

"I did keep buying him wine all evening. I don't know why he didn't drink it."

> *Fuzzy Zoeller, on having dinner with Greg Norman the night before they were to face each other in a playoff at the '84 U.S. Open*

POLITICS

"I can't think of a better way to spend a morning with somebody than riding around a golf course, letting 'em win."

> *Steve Eure, Washington lobbyist, on playing golf with politicians*

"I write on airplanes. It's my version of golf, a way of breaking out, thinking differently."
Newt Gingrich

"The golf grip is a lot like politics. If you hold the club too far to the right, you're going to get in trouble on the left. If you hold it too far to the left, you're going to have trouble from the right. But if you hold it in the middle. . . ."
Tom Watson, advice he gave to
President Clinton

POOR

"In my day you drank milk with a fork because you didn't want that milk to run out."
Chi Chi Rodriguez

"I came from such a poor family, my sister was made in Japan."
Lee Trevino

"A lot of guys on the tour gripe about losing their laundry. . . . And I remember when I only had one shirt."

Lee Trevino

PRACTICE
MAKES PERFECT

"If you're playing good, why do you need to practice? If you aren't hitting it good, what good will it do to practice a bad swing?"

Fred Couples

"Practice always took the zip out of me anyway. I preferred to be keen, fresh, and eager when play actually started."

Walter Hagen

"We can make 100 putts in a row on the putting green, but you have to take it to the golf course. That's when it becomes mental."

Mike Hulbert, sympathizing with Shaquille O'Neal, who hits most of his free throws in practice but has trouble during the game

"There are no secrets to golf. The secret of success is practice—constant but intelligent practice."
Ernest Jones

"Practice is the only golf advice that is good for everybody."
Arnold Palmer

"There is no such thing as natural touch. Touch is something you create by hitting millions of golf balls."
Lee Trevino

"I'm the damn U.S. Open champion. What do you expect, lady, ground balls?"
Lee Trevino, to a woman oohing and aahing at Trevino's practice shots

PRESSURE POINT

"Pressure is when you've got to putt for money and the only money you've got is your ball marker."
George Archer

"It's like driving on ice. You've got both hands on the wheel and you can't stop."

John Huston, on pressure

"I wish I could do a Vulcan Mind Meld here so you could feel it."

*Peter Jacobsen, trying to explain
the pressure of having to hit a
three-footer at the Ryder Cup*

"One always feels that he is running from something without knowing what nor where it is."

*Bobby Jones, on the pressure of
major championships*

"I would rather open on Broadway in *Hamlet* with no rehearsals than tee off at Pebble Beach."

Jack Lemmon

"I almost threw up on myself. . . . I could not breathe. There was no saliva in my mouth."

*Davis Love III, on a key putt in the
'83 Ryder Cup*

"I shot a wild elephant in Africa thirty yards from me, and it didn't hit the ground until it was right at my feet. I wasn't a bit scared. But a four-foot putt scares me to death."

Sam Snead

"Pressure is playing for $50 with a guy with a scar on his cheek when you only got $2 in your pocket."

Lee Trevino

"When you're playing for $500 and you have to borrow a penny to spot your ball, now that's pressure."

Lee Trevino

NICK PRICE

"You can't have your A game every week. If you did, you'd play like Nick Price."

Jim Gallagher, Jr.

"Price is longer than Tolstoy."

Rick Reilly, on Nick Price

PRO TOUR

"I'm so happy to be on the Tour, a little speck in the history of sports."
Mac O'Grady

PUTTERS

"I either give 'em away or they die an ugly death."
Ken Green, on throwing eight putters into the lake after bad putts

"I discovered that when you one-putt greens your score goes down."
Peter Jacobsen, on shooting a 64 with a new putter

"I don't want a putter to get to know me too well."
Lee Trevino, on changing putters all the time

"I've gone through more putters than Carter's has pills."

Tom Watson

"I got tired of looking at the old one. It's like a pair of shoes. You look at 'em and look at 'em and pretty soon you're tired of looking at 'em."

Fuzzy Zoeller, on using a new putter after three years

PUTTING

"The putt is the dullest, most time-consuming, and worst-handled part of golf. On television, it comes through like an appendectomy."

Furman Bisher

"Every putt can go in, but I don't expect every putt to go in."

Jane Blalock

"One, two, three, four."

Mark Brooks, asked to describe a four-putt he had at the U.S. Open

"Bad putting stems from thinking how instead of where."

Jackie Burke, Jr.

"It's really been a humiliating experience."

President George Bush, on putting

"Putting and fishing are two of the things I hate the most."

George Bush

"Actually, I think my putting is one of the reasons I'm more calm now than I used to be—the discipline that comes from being a lousy putter."

George Bush

"It's unfortunate, but I win tournaments because I putt well, and I lose them because I don't."

Fred Couples

"If it's my day, they go in, and on a bad day, they won't."

Laura Davies, on her putting philosophy

"I'd putt sitting up in a coffin if I thought I could hole something."

Gardner Dickinson

"Whoever makes the putts wins. If you don't, you finish 20th."

Ken Green

"There are two games of golf. One is the game of golf, the other is putting."

Ben Hogan

"You're thinking that you're going to miss the hole, you're going to drop the putter, you're going to whiff on the ball, anything."

Peter Jacobsen, describing what goes on in his mind when he has to hit a clutch two-foot putt

"Why didn't I win more? I was the world's worst putter."

Wild Bill Mehlhorn

"You have about as much chance of winning a lottery as making the putt you flinch at or walk away from."

Jim Murray

"Missing a short putt is about the most humiliating thing in the world, because you're supposed to make them."

Byron Nelson

"I missed so many putts out there, I was afraid to eat lunch for fear I'd miss my mouth."

Harold Paddock, after shooting 84 in the first round of the '66 PGA

"Putting is like wisdom—partly a natural gift and partly the accumulation of experience."

Arnold Palmer

"Maybe when you're away from bad putting for three months, you forget how to do it."

Jesper Parnevik, on explaining why he was playing very well after a three-month break

"Oh, yes, I have. I'm often short with my long putts."

> *Horton Smith, winner of the first Masters, responding to observations that he seemed to have no vices*

QUALIFIERS

"You wind up hoping for nasty weather or a flu bug, or anything that keeps guys away and gets you into the tournaments."

> *Emlyn Aubrey, on his status as one of 25 pros who do not get a full exemption on the Tour*

"They called me the king of the minitours. Out here I feel like a pawn."

> *Dick Mast, on playing in the U.S. Open*

"I'm broke and I don't want to get a job. All I own are a Porsche and a suntan."

> *Lance Ten Broeck, after failing to qualify for the PGA Tour*

RECORDS

"Do you know how hard it is to write 59? I've written 69 three times by mistake."

Al Geiberger, on signing autographs after shooting his record-setting 59

"It's like . . . personally scoring six touchdowns in an afternoon against Notre Dame."

Jim Murray, on Al Geiberger's record 59

RELAXATION TECHNIQUES

"The pace of living is so fast today that a golf course is one of the last places to watch a squirrel climb a tree."

Jackie Burke, Sr., on the importance of being relaxed at a golf course

"I'm very relaxed when I'm playing, because it's not a job. It's a game."

Nancy Lopez

RELIGION

"I've played many rounds with Billy. We're a lot alike. He prays and I cheat."

Bob Hope, on playing golf with
Billy Graham

"Some people say I look like I'm praying."

Fuzzy Zoeller, on his swinging style

RETIREMENT

"Doing very little and getting very good at it."

Hubert Green, asked what he had
done during a several-year break
before joining the Senior Tour

"I'm making the longest farewell tour since the Grateful Dead."

Charlie Mechem, on retiring as
LPGA commissioner

"If we get together too often, we'll remember what it was we didn't like about each other."

> *Cary Middlecoff, early in his*
> *Senior Tour career, on the many*
> *tournaments he was playing*

"I don't think Jack and I have ever played together without playing one another."

> *Arnold Palmer, on being cognizant of*
> *Nicklaus even though they were both*
> *well behind in the Masters*

"We know each other very well, we know each other's game very well. Mike knows that I can probably club him as well as anybody."

> *Lee Trevino, on he and Mike Hill*
> *being paired at the Legends of*
> *Golf tournament*

RIVIERA GOLF CLUB
(CALIFORNIA)

"Very nice course. But tell me, where do the members play?"

Bobby Jones

ROUGHS

"You know if you get grass stains on your knuckles hitting a pitch shot, the artistry has been eliminated."

Roger Maltbie, on deep roughs around the greens

"The man who can go into a patch of rough alone, with the knowledge that only God is watching him, and play his ball where it lies, is the man who will serve you faithfully and well."

P. G. Wodehouse

"There is no sport like golf, where the players make the long walk up the 18th fairway and the cheer becomes a wave of deafening noise. It is a triumphant march normally reserved for royalty."

Jack Berry, sportswriter,
Detroit News

"Sorry, I don't play golf while on vacation."

Ben Hogan, asked when vacationing in France if he would like to play golf with the King of Belgium

"The Beatles got one below my level."

Tony Jacklin, on being given the title of an Officer of the British Empire by the Queen after winning the British Open

"Golf always makes me so damned angry."

King George V

RULES

"I got a contract from Rolex."

>*Seve Ballesteros, on the only good*
>*thing that came out of his being*
>*disqualified from the '80 U.S. Open*
>*for showing up seven minutes late*

"You have to play the rules of golf just as you have
to live by the rules of life. There's no other way."
>*Babe Didrikson*

RYDER CUP

"Play bloody well."

>*Nick Faldo, advice he would give to*
>*a Ryder Cup rookie*

"You're just playing for a trophy and you end up
lying on the floor shattered. It's quite amazing
what you go through."

>*Nick Faldo, on the impact of the*
>*Ryder Cup*

"Free clothes."

> *Brad Faxon, on why he tried so hard*
> *to make the Ryder Cup team*

"Win, and you are the supreme beings in all the universe. Lose, and may the fleas of a million rodents infect your every orifice."

> *David Feherty, on the pressure of the*
> *Ryder Cup*

"We could play 100 holes and we would not be tired. The spectators will carry us in their arms."

> *Ignacio Garrido, on the fans rooting*
> *on the European team at the '97*
> *Ryder Cup*

"If you don't want to play your heart out for the good old red, white, and blue, you've got no business on the team."

> *Dave Marr, on the Ryder Cup*

"A regular tour event is a 35-foot dive off a cliff, a major is a 50-foot dive, and the Ryder Cup is a 100-foot dive."

> *Johnny Miller*

"I've been on a winning, losing, and tying team—and to tell you the truth, I didn't have fun on any of them."

> Mark O'Meara, on the pressure of the Ryder Cup

"Why did you send Seve there? He cried more than me."

> Costantino Rocca, on Bernard Gallacher, then Ryder Cup captain, sending in Seve Ballesteros to try to cheer up Rocca after he missed a key putt

"I am an American in Europe. I have to put a bag over my head."

> Dan Shaughnessy, Boston Globe columnist, on the European team's upset of the American team at the '97 Ryder Cup in Spain

"We went over there to win, not to be good ol' boys."

> Sam Snead, on being angry at Jack Nicklaus for conceding a putt to Tony Jacklin that resulted in a tie at the '69 Ryder Cup

"I had tears in my eyes and goose bumps. . . . You felt that you wanted to come out fighting and swinging like Rocky."

> *Curtis Strange, on his first Ryder Cup in 1983*

"We're even cheering for Ken Green."

> *Curtis Strange, on the enthusiasm of a U.S. Ryder Cup team*

"They criticized me because they couldn't beat nobody. When I put them up against a bulldog, what do they want, the Chihuahua?"

> *Lee Trevino, on being captain of the U.S. Ryder Cup team and being criticized by players after they lost*

"We are friends. We are not at war here. They're not issuing grenades and rifles. It's a golf match."

> *Lee Trevino, on people taking the Ryder Cup too seriously*

"I could feel the hair standing on the back of my head, and then my right leg started shaking."

> *Philip Walton, on hitting the winning putt in the '95 Ryder Cup for Europe*

"This is the only event in the world that will make your legs shake."

Tom Watson

"It's about nerve . . . who's got it and who ain't."

Ian Woosnam, on Europe winning the Ryder Cup

SECOND PLACE

"I just play pitiful golf today. But I finish second. That's not too bad first time U.S. Open."

T. C. Chen, on losing the '85 U.S. Open on the last day with an 8 on the 5th hole

"It would seem that if you fell off a turnip truck seven times, you'd land on the grass instead of the asphalt at least once."

Hale Irwin, on seven seconds in his first year on the Senior Tour

"You could have shot off an elephant gun in my corner of the room and not winged a single sportswriter."

> *Sam Snead, on finishing second to*
> *Ralph Guldahl at the '37 U.S. Open*

"As a runner-up, I was nothin'."

> *Sam Snead, after losing to Guldahl*
> *at the 1939 U.S. Open*

"You don't come out here and blow these guys' doors off. They're too good. And you can't hate yourself for finishing second."

> *Fuzzy Zoeller*

SENIOR TOUR

"What ticks me off is seeing how much the seniors are making playing on Mickey Mouse golf courses, shooting 20 under par."

> *Helen Alfredsson, on the disparity*
> *between the Senior Tour and*
> *the LPGA*

"My knees are only a few months old, my back is only 17, and I recently got a new hip. I might be too young now."

George Archer, on his qualifications for playing the Senior Tour

"It's a hard way to make an easy living."

Jerry Barber, at age 74, while still playing on the Senior Tour

"One of the perks of senior golf is that you get to come back as anybody you want."

Thomas Boswell, on senior golfers changing personas from their prior golf careers

"I used to be known as a grouch and a grump. Look at me now. Wearing knickers and silly hats. I never thought I'd see the day."

Billy Casper

"In some cases the good old days were never this good."

Billy Casper, on how much he enjoys the Senior Tour

"When oil started selling for $10 a barrel instead of $44 a barrel, I got the old putter out."

> *Bruce Crampton, on joining the Senior Tour after retiring from golf to go into the oil business*

"I'm in the wrong league. I can't wait for those seniors."

> *Ray Floyd, at age 48, after shooting a 68 in the first round of a tournament and still being six shots behind the leader*

"On this tour, you don't get better as you get older. On the regular tour, you get better as you get older."

> *Al Geiberger, on most seniors winning tournaments between the ages of 50 and 55*

"If I didn't need the money, my rear wouldn't be out here."

> *Dave Hill, on the Senior Tour*

"I've got to get my licks in, then go back and play where I'm supposed to play."

> *Hale Irwin, at age 50, warming up for the Masters*

"On the regular tour if you miss a shot, 50 guys go by you. Miss two shots and 100 guys go by you. Here, at least, you can count the ones that go past you."

> *Hale Irwin, on the Senior Tour*

"I'm going to have to talk to the government about his visa."

> *Don January, on the hot play of Australian Peter Thomson, who had five Senior Tour victories in 1985*

"I do it for the money, plain and simple. It keeps me going."

> *Don January, on the Senior Tour*

"The game is very elusive. I can't believe I could ever play it."

> *Dave Marr, on the Senior Tour*

"You shouldn't have two tees. If you're going to do that, they ought to make us ride in carts and wear petticoats."

> *Arnold Palmer, on the 1989*
> *Tournament of Champions, where*
> *seniors and regulars played together*
> *and the tees were moved up for*
> *the seniors*

"Sometimes I feel like Secretariat. I can come from behind and win, or I can hold a lead."

> *Chi Chi Rodriguez, on his success on*
> *the Senior Tour*

"All I know is that my 40th birthday was a lot harder than my 50th."

> *Chi Chi Rodriguez, on enjoying the*
> *Senior Tour*

"Some of these guys wouldn't pour water on you if you were on fire."

> *J. C. Snead, claiming that Senior*
> *Tour players are not as nice as is*
> *commonly thought*

"We're playing for the money. Don't think we're playing for the camaraderie. It's getting pretty expensive."

> *Sam Snead, soon after the formation of the Senior Tour*

"They could put my locker in where they keep the urinals, it wouldn't matter to me."

> *Tom Wargo, Senior Tour player, on how much being on the tour meant to him*

SHARK

"He can hit it higher than Superman can fly."

> *Hubert Green, on Greg Norman*

"The only difference between my game and Greg Norman's is 75 yards off the tee."

> *Hale Irwin*

"About like a ten-foot alligator chasin' you."

> *Larry Mize, asked how he felt about being just ahead of Greg Norman at the Masters*

"He doesn't look like a guy you'd want to cheat at cards or make a pass at his girlfriend or steal his wallet."

> *Jim Murray, on the rugged good looks of Norman*

"He's not the most talented guy, but the sinews of character and determination within him are really amazing."

> *Mac O'Grady, on Norman*

"He's the White Shark and I'm the loan shark."

> *Chi Chi Rodriguez, kidding around with Norman*

"Greg Norman can hit a tennis ball 300 yards. Hell, he can hit a plum 250 yards."

> *Lee Trevino*

PATTY SHEEHAN

"The best sign of how good Patty is, is that she hasn't changed putters during her career."

> *Meg Mallon, on Patty Sheehan's reputation as a top putter*

"There are no holes where you can think, 'Hey, man, rest here.'"

> *John Daly, on Shinnecock being*
> *one of the toughest courses he has*
> *ever played*

"If it was human, it would have teeth missing and tattoos, a gun in its belt, and murder in its heart."
> *Jim Murray*

"They used plows and mules and shovels and built one heck of a golf course."
> *Lee Trevino*

"If the wind didn't blow, I thought they'd need the fire department out here to keep us from burning it up. But with or without the wind, this course can eat your lunch."
> *Lee Trevino*

"I'm just lucky I didn't break any bones. This course will wear you out."

> *Fuzzy Zoeller, after shooting a 76 at Shinnecock Hills*

SHOT HEARD 'ROUND THE WORLD

"The aspect I cherish most is that both Walter Hagen and Bobby Jones witnessed the shot."

> *Gene Sarazen, on one of golf's most famous shots, his double eagle in the '35 Masters*

SHOT IN THE DARK

"That one didn't suffer. It was dead before it hit the ground."

> *David Feherty, on a bad shot by Dennis Franz at a pro-am tournament*

"That's what we call a Marge Schott—just a little bit to the right."

> *Gary McCord, on a bad shot*

SCOTT SIMPSON

"What's boring when you shoot scores that beat everybody else's?"

> *Bob Gilder, on those who call Scott Simpson a boring golfer*

"If he were a pitcher, he would be known for his control. He wouldn't walk anybody. But he wouldn't strike out anybody either."

> *Jim Murray, on Scott Simpson*

SKATING WARS

"I've got 14 clubs and a 318-pound caddie. Are you kidding?"

> *Lee Trevino, asked if he was scared after the Tonya Harding–Nancy Kerrigan incident*

"I've always said Sam Snead could balance the U.S. budget, as smart as he is about money."

Fred Corcoran, Snead's manager

"Sam Snead is one of a handful of golfers who inspire the club players with the conviction that golf is easy."

Peter Dobereiner

"They say Sam Snead is a natural golfer. But if he didn't practice, he'd be a natural bad golfer."

Gary Player

"Jack Nicklaus was second."

Sam Snead, asked on his 85th birthday who the greatest golfer of all time was

SLICE

"Hook it."

> *Jimmy Demaret, advice he gave to*
> *someone who asked him how to get*
> *rid of his slice*

SLUMPS

"The last couple of years have confirmed what I know: that I have few friends, many acquaintances, very many enemies."

> *Seve Ballesteros, on going through*
> *a slump*

"I got contact lenses so I could see. Now I can see I can't make anything.

> *Jack Nicklaus, on a slump*

"I've got a lot of tournaments left, but you have to ask yourself, is that a plus or a minus? It's a lot like the Cubs. They have a lot of games left, but is that good or bad?"

> *David Ogrin, touring pro, on a*
> *bad year*

J. C. SNEAD

"Don't tell anybody. You'll screw up my image."

> *J. C. Snead, after being told by a*
> *reporter that he thought Snead was a*
> *good guy*

SPIRO IS MY HERO

"It may be of value to these golf fans who plan to attend the next Bob Hope Desert Classic—to know that I intend to participate. Check the guest list before you venture out."

> *Spiro Agnew, after the former vice*
> *president hit fans two years in a row*
> *at the Desert Classic*

"I have some that say 'You have just been hit by . . .' and then I sign it."

> *Spiro Agnew, on a golf ball given to him by President Nixon*

"Palm Springs is going to be known as Agnew's Fault."

> *Bob Hope, after Agnew hit three people in his first two shots at Palm Springs, just days after an earthquake struck the area*

"You never have to count his score. Just count his casualties."

> *Bob Hope, on Agnew*

"When Agnew yelled 'fore,' you never knew whether he was telling someone to get out of the way or if he was predicting how many spectators he would hit with the shot."

> *Bob Hope*

"A Spiro Special."

> *Johnny Miller, after shanking a shot at the Crosby Pro-Am and almost hitting someone in the crowd*

"I'll give you a golf ball. It's for putting only."
> *Richard Nixon, to Agnew, before presenting him with a special golf ball bearing the presidential seal*

CURTIS STRANGE

"Anytime he's near the lead, he's gonna win."
> *Mark O'Meara, on the clutch play of Curtis Strange*

STRATEGY

"I just hit the hell out of it."
> *Chi Chi Rodriguez, on his strategy for hitting the ball*

"I've hit a million and a half golf balls in my time, and I've had a plan in my mind for every one of 'em."
> *Sam Snead*

SUPER SENIORS

"The Super Seniors have given me a niche. But if I had to beat Hale Irwin every week, I'd go home."
Don January, on the Super Senior Tour (over age 60)

"We're going to have a Super Super Super Super Super Seniors. If you win when you're 95, you get a thirty-year exemption."
Lee Trevino

SWING TIME

"It doesn't matter if you look like a beast before or after the hit, as long as you look like a beauty at the moment of impact."
Seve Ballesteros

"I just threw junk up there."
Julius Boros, describing his golf technique

"Doing everything that, as a country club pro, I tell my students not to do."

> Ed Furgol, on his unorthodox
> swinging style, the result of a broken
> arm he suffered as a child

"I figure I went from having a funny swing to a classic one."

> Hubert Green, after Ben Hogan told
> him he had a good swing

"The Tour today is a production line of ramp-model golf swings. They're very pretty to watch, but also spiritually undernourished."

> Gary McCord

"Learning to play or making a swing change is like running 26 times with your head down into a brick wall. After a while you sit back and say, 'What am I doing this for?'"

> Gary McCord

"I don't care what a guy swings like. If he can make the same swing every time, he can score."

> Byron Nelson

"Nobody I've seen has a swing that works for every club in the bag."

Sam Snead

"I try to feel oily."

Sam Snead, describing how he stays loose when he swings

"The average player is too anxious to see good results on the scoreboard before she has fully absorbed the principles of the golf swing in mind and muscle on the practice tee."

Louise Suggs

"No matter how powerful your engine, you must have gradual acceleration of speed. So it is in a golf swing."

Mickey Wright

"I wrapped these knuckles on an 8-iron and said, 'Where the hell's it going this time?'"

Fuzzy Zoeller, on his swinging philosophy

TALK TOO MUCH

"Ben talks to me on every hole. When we go to the green he always says, 'You're away.'"

> *Jimmy Demaret, refuting stories*
> *that Hogan never talked during a*
> *golf match*

"Not much, except for me to say, 'Nice putt.'"

> *Jack Nicklaus, asked if he spoke*
> *much to his partner, Isao Aoki, at the*
> *U.S. Open*

"I always regret what I say. Anyone who talks as much as I do has to say something wrong."

> *Lee Trevino*

TEE SHOTS

"You don't get bad bounces in the air."

> *Chi Chi Rodriguez, on using a high*
> *tee for his shots*

"Don't pick up your tee so fast. Stand there and admire it."

> *Lee Trevino, advice he gave to*
> *football star Emmitt Smith after*
> *Smith's long tee shot*

TEMPER, TEMPER

"I just looked like I ought to throw clubs."

> *Tommy Bolt, on his legendary temper*

"You should be allowed to go over into the woods to eliminate a whole set of clubs if you don't like them."

> *Tommy Bolt, on throwing clubs*

"I guess I do have a pretty low boiling point, but I haven't broken nearly as many clubs as people think. Only a dozen or so."

> *Tommy Bolt*

"One bad shot deserves another."

> *Tommy Bolt, on his temper*

"When you lose your temper after missing a shot, the chances are you will miss the next shot, too."
Julius Boros

"When I first started playing I never threw my clubs, because I couldn't afford it."
Larry Nelson, on being
even-tempered on the golf course

TENNIS, ANYONE?

"In golf, you miss your first three shots and it ruins your whole day. In tennis, it is just love–40."
Pete Burwash, tennis commentator

"That was five times worse than playing in a Wimbledon final."
Ivan Lendl, after getting an
exemption to play at a European
PGA Tour event and missing the cut
by 15 strokes

"If I had to play a third set, I would have missed nine holes."

> *Ivan Lendl, on why he was happy to win a best two-of-three match in two straight sets*

"There are no bad calls."

> *Ivan Lendl, on why he loves golf*

"Grass isn't his best surface."

> *Roger Maltbie, on Lendl hitting five balls into a water hazard in a celebrity tournament*

"My short game in golf is bad, but it's pretty good in tennis."

> *Wendy Turnbull*

TIGER

"He's Michael Jordan in long pants."

> *Paul Azinger, on Tiger Woods*

"Whether in the majors or at the Ryder Cup, everything swirled around him. He was El Niño."

> Tom Callahan, on the impact of Tiger
> Woods's first year on the pro tour

"If he keeps playing the way he is playing and you win a tournament [and] he is not there, you need an asterisk next to your name."

> Brad Faxon

"Never has my flabber been so completely gasted. He is the longest hitter I've ever seen."

> David Feherty

"I said I wish I had an opportunity to work for him."

> Peter Jacobsen, on losing his
> longtime caddie, Mike "Fluff"
> Cowan, to Tiger Woods

"He looks pretty happy being the first Tiger. Just let him be the first Tiger."

> Michael Jordan, on Tiger Woods being
> called the Michael Jordan of golf

"It's Tiger Woods against the world, and the world doesn't have a chance."

Vartan Kupelian, Detroit News
sportswriter

"It's almost like trying to hold off the inevitable, like bailing water out of a sinking ship."

Tom Lehman, on Tiger Woods closing in on Lehman at a tournament

"The only way he could have hit it [the ball] faster is if one of the Cubs' pitchers were pitching to him."

Jay Leno, on Tiger Woods's driving ability

"It's like talking about Babe Ruth or Einstein or Tiger Woods."

George Lucas, asked to describe the talents of Steven Spielberg

"I appreciated that he hit the ball long and straight, and I appreciated his iron shots were very accurate. I did not appreciate how well he putted."

Colin Montgomerie, on Woods

"What do you mean what makes me say that? Have you been on holiday? Did you just get here?"

> *Colin Montgomerie, after saying*
> *that it would be impossible to catch*
> *Tiger Woods, who held an 11-shot*
> *lead, heading into the final round*
> *of the Masters*

"Tiger is playing another game. He's playing a golf course he'll own for a long time."

> *Jack Nicklaus, on the Masters*

"He's more dominant over the guys he's playing against than I ever was on the ones I played against."

> *Jack Nicklaus*

"He makes the golf course into nothing. If he plays well, the golf course becomes nothing."

> *Jack Nicklaus, on Tiger*

"It's great. Nobody will ever be able to criticize the rest of us for finishing second anymore."

> *Greg Norman*

"He seems to project a certain aura of punctuated arrogance."

Mac O'Grady, on Tiger at age 16

"I had to use binoculars to see how far the ball was going."

Jose-Maria Olazabal

"Sometimes it feels like you're invisible out there."

Mark O'Meara, on sharing a first-round lead with Tiger at a Tour event

"Unless they build Tiger tees about 50 yards back, he's going to win the next 20 of them."

Jesper Parnevik, on the Masters

"He is going to be able to do some things on golf courses most of us dream about."

Nick Price

"I wish he would have stayed in school and got his Ph.D."

Jeff Sluman

"I might have a chance if I make five or six birdies in the first two or three holes."

> *Paul Stankowski, on being behind*
> *Woods by 10 strokes at the Masters*

"He may be the type of player that comes around once in a millennium."

> *Tom Watson, on Tiger*

TREES

"One guy in Montana approached me about a Christmas tree farm ad, but he never got back to me."

> *Lon Hinkle, asked if he ever*
> *capitalized on his shot in the '79 U.S.*
> *Open where he figured out a way of*
> *circumventing a tree, a feat that*
> *resulted in USGA officials having to*
> *hurriedly plant a tree to prevent it*
> *from happening again*

"If your husband had to play the courses he designed, you'd be on bread lines."

> *Ben Hogan, said to the wife of*
> *Robert Trent Jones*

"Never mind the people. Just move this tree a few feet to the left."

> *Jack Nicklaus, asked if he wanted*
> *the crowd moved after his tee shot*
> *ended up near a tree*

LEE TREVINO

"What am I supposed to do? Trade him for Lee Trevino?"

> *Bobby Clarke, Philadelphia Flyers*
> *GM, on hockey player Todd Bergen*
> *wanting to pursue a career as*
> *a golfer*

"He's the only man I've ever known who talks on his backswing."

> *Charley McClendon, former LSU*
> *football coach, on playing golf*
> *with Trevino*

"There's a new sheriff in town."

> *Herman Mitchell, Trevino's caddie,*
> *on Trevino turning 50 and joining*
> *the Senior Tour*

"The guy can do drawings with a golf ball. He looks like Pablo Picasso out there."

Chi Chi Rodriguez, on Trevino

"When you're smarter than most guys and you just work harder than most guys, what more do you need?"

Dave Stockton, on the work ethic of Trevino

"Trevino has more lines than the L & N railroad."

Fuzzy Zoeller, on Trevino's sense of humor

U.S. OPEN

"That's a performance for which no one ever need apologize."

Billy Casper, on beating Arnold Palmer at the '66 U.S. Open and Palmer apologizing to fans even though he shot a last-round 71

"When you're a little kid and you're putting, you don't always think about making a putt for the Westchester Classic."

Fred Couples, on the U.S. Open

"There are more bogeys in the last nine holes of the U.S. Open than in any other tournament in God's creation."

Raymond Floyd

"All of a sudden I'm an expert on everything. Interviewers want your opinion on golf, foreign policy, and the price of peanuts."

Hubert Green, on winning the U.S. Open

"Anybody can win the Open once."

Walter Hagen

"Nobody ever wins an Open. Everybody else just loses it."

Bobby Jones

"I was flipping like a hot fish on a grill."

Tom Kite, on his sleeplessness before the U.S. Open final round

"No sports event in the world can mean as much to its winner—in prestige, in money, in just plain ego satisfaction—as the U.S. Open."

Tony Lema

"Did he play every hole?"

Bobby Locke, after Ben Hogan shot a final-round 67 on the last day of the '51 Open

"You come within a putt of winning, and two years later you have to qualify. I love it. That's why it's called the U.S. Open, not closed."

Mark McCumber, who was second in the U.S. Open in '89 and had to qualify in '91

"The Open is the Holy Grail of those knights of the round green."

Jim Murray

"If the Open were a world war, Albania would win it."

Jim Murray, on the U.S. Open being the home of the underdog

"They come into an Open like guys in chains. They know it's going to be four days of silent screaming. . . . The rack."

Jim Murray, on Open contestants

"Oh, to be young and not know what this game is all about."

Byron Nelson, on young Rives McBee shooting a 64 in the second round of the '66 Open

"An Open is not really only a measure of how you handle a golf course, it's a measure of how you handle yourself—how patient you are, how experienced you are."

Jack Nicklaus

"You can't win the Open on Thursday and Friday, but you can lose it."

Jack Nicklaus

"The Open wins. The winner merely survives."

Gary Nuhn, Dayton Daily News

"It would be a tribute to the American spirit if I triumphed on Sunday."

> *Mac O'Grady, on being suspended and then coming back to be in close contention for the '86 U.S. Open*

"I make sure that I don't play for a couple of weeks before the tournament so that the lymphatic system in the brain that stores all the emotional memory circuits has a couple of weeks of rest."

> *Mac O'Grady, on prepping for the U.S. Open*

"Like being on the shuttle with the O-rings about to go."

> *Mac O'Grady, on the pressure of being in contention in the final round of the U.S. Open*

"It was as though the Man upstairs said, 'Sam, we gave you a lot, but we're not going to let you have a full plate.'"

> *Sam Snead, on never winning the U.S. Open*

"Right score, wrong time."

> *Sam Snead, after shooting a 3 a week after he lost the U.S. Open, at the same course, by shooting an 8*

"If you don't have it when you get here, don't expect to find it here."

> *Sam Snead, on players who work on their golf swing at the U.S. Open*

"I was due to collect money for endorsing everything from corn planters to flea powder."

> *Sam Snead, on leading the '37 U.S. Open before Ralph Guldahl made his phenomenal last-minute move to win*

"The U.S. Open is the San Quentin of golf. You don't so much play it as try to escape from it. Nobody beats the U.S. Open; you survive it."

> *Art Spander*

"You know something is up when you have a knot in your stomach for a week."

> *Curtis Strange, on preparation for the U.S. Open*

"We want to provide as legitimate a test as we can to identify the best golfer in the world that week. Nothing else. We're not running a penal institution."

Buzz Taylor, USGA Championship Committee chair, on players complaining about how difficult the U.S. Open is to play

"I thought I'd blown it when I drove it into that trap. God is a Mexican."

Lee Trevino, after winning the '72 Open with a phenomenal shot from the bunker on the 17th hole

"People who have won it have achieved perfection or scrambled like a magician."

Tom Watson

"Being at the Open is like Christmastime. I always get excited around Christmas. It's the same around the Open. I get excited because it's the Open."

Tom Watson

"It takes courage to win the U.S. Open, more courage than it takes for any other tournament."

Tom Watson

"The leader board is so rich, if it were food, we'd all have acne."

> *Jack Whitaker, on many big-name players near the lead going into the final round of the '87 U.S. Open*

"We've had a few U.S. Opens that didn't leave the ground, and that was one of them."

> *Herbert Warren Wind, on the '75 U.S. Open, won by Lou Graham, who bested John Mahaffey in a playoff*

VALDERRAMA (SPAIN)

"You have to play like God out there to shoot par."
> *Nick Faldo*

"The 511-yard 17th . . . has undergone so many face-lifts that it has become known as the Michael Jackson of golf holes."
> *Dan Jenkins*

HARRY VARDON

"I cannot believe that anyone ever had or will have a greater genius for hitting a golf ball than Harry Vardon."

Bernard Darwin

TOM WATSON

"If I'm playing Tom Watson, I know I have to win. With somebody else against you, maybe you feel they'll lose instead."

Jack Nicklaus, on Watson

WEATHER OUTSIDE IS FRIGHTFUL

"It was hideous. Even the crows were walking."

Howard Clark, on a torrential
rainstorm at St. Andrews

"Hell can't be any hotter. I'm checking that out one of these days."

> *Ben Hogan, on 100-degree*
> *temperatures at the U.S. Open in*
> *New Jersey*

"You realize if Chicago had weather, it would be scary."

> *Peter Jacobsen, on Chicago being a*
> *great place to play on those rare*
> *good-weather days*

"The kind the Scots call a refreshing breeze and Americans call a grab-on-to-a-fence-or-get-blown-to-Denmark."

> *Dan Jenkins, on the winds during the*
> *first round of the '97 British Open*

"Last year, if we had had these winds, with as hard as the greens were, we would still be playing in the '88 tournament right now."

> *Tom Kite, on miserable conditions*
> *during the second round of the*
> *'89 Masters*

"But if you figure the windchill factor, it's only 102."

> *Dave Marr, on a 104-degree day at the U.S. Women's Open*

"If you want to make a change, call up God and have the weather changed."

> *Arnold Palmer, asked if the Masters should be changed in any way*

"Funny thing, I'll bet I done won me more tournaments in swamps than in sunshine."

> *Sam Snead, on his dislike of rain*

"I guess I'm a mudder."

> *Craig Stadler, on shooting a 66 in the rain at the '79 Masters*

"I'm from Texas, and this isn't heat. Heck, I should have worn all black today."

> *Rocky Thompson, on a 90-degree day at a seniors tournament in Michigan*

"There's never any plus side to having heat like this unless you live in Alaska in December."

*Lee Trevino, on playing a
tournament in 100-degree heat*

"This is a tournament for flat bellies. A stubby guy like me gets wrapped up in a sweater and can't take a full backswing. I need all the swing I can get."

*Lee Trevino, on cool weather at a
PGA tournament*

"Let's play in the Philippines."

*Lee Trevino, suggesting the U.S.
Open be moved since he plays so well
in the rain*

"It don't move, but it's trying to."

*Art Wall, on the movement of his
golf ball during gale-force winds
at the Masters*

"More suitable to hunting caribou than playing golf."

*Herbert Warren Wind, on frigid
conditions at the U.S. Open at
Hazeltine in Minnesota*

"Thanks to Michigan for trying to show us four different seasons in one day."

> *Fuzzy Zoeller, on bizarre weather conditions at the '85 U.S. Open at Oakland Hills in Michigan*

"It wasn't a Chamber of Commerce day."

> *Fuzzy Zoeller, on miserable weather during the first round of the '86 U.S. Open at Shinnecock Hills on Long Island*

WEIGHTY ISSUES

"A mile? With that belly, you'd have a better chance running for governor."

> *Chi Chi Rodriguez, after Lee Trevino told him he was going to run a mile*

"I thought if I took him past dinnertime, I'd have him. I guess I was wrong."

> *Jim Simon, on a playoff ending at the 6th hole of the Greater Hartford Open, where Simon lost to 6'6", 225-pound Howard Twitty*

"My weight must've just shifted or my feet are bigger."

> *Craig Stadler, on being told by*
> *several people that he lost weight*

"When a man weighs 295 pounds, you have to give him some opportunity to make his legs and muscles move, and golf offers that opportunity."

> *President William Howard Taft*

"If I don't [lose 20 pounds] then I am just going to eat me some tacos and drink me some Crystal Light and the hell with it."

> *Lee Trevino*

"Do you realize that between us, we've lost Laura Baugh?"

> *Stan Wood, former USC golf coach*
> *who lost 50 pounds, to JoAnne*
> *Carner, who had lost 45 pounds*

"He is tall, good-looking, he hits the ball far, putts well, and he has a pretty wife."

Ben Crenshaw, at age 18, explaining why Weiskopf was his favorite player on the pro tour

"Weiskopf has as much or more talent than Nicklaus. He just wasn't as interested."

Lee Trevino

WHAT'S IN A NAME?

"They had money. I'm not akin to that group. I'm more familiar with the Samuel Adams brewery."

John Adams, pro golfer, asked if he was related to the former president

"Maybe a ringer can win it."

Ray Floyd, on Jim Ringer, a relative unknown, leading the U.S. Senior Open

"I'm not an unknown—everyone in my family knows me."

> *Ken Green, on being the first-round leader of the '86 Masters*

"My name used to be O'Conner, but I changed it for business reasons."

> *Chi Chi Rodriguez*

"I feel more like Homer Simpson."

> *Scott Simpson, after faltering on the last three holes the third day after leading the '90 U.S. Open*

"We call him 'I lost the ball.' Unfortunately, he hasn't lost enough balls. He's a great player."

> *Tom Watson, on the best way to pronounce the last name of Jose-Maria Olazabal*

KATHY WHITWORTH

"When she had to putt, she got it every time."

> *Sandra Haynie, on the great putting skills of Kathy Whitworth*

WINGED FOOT (NEW YORK)

"Putting on those greens is like playing miniature golf without the board."
Hale Irwin

WINNING

"I gave hope to every golfer in the world."
Brad Bryant, on posting the first win of his 18-year career

"Keep your head up. Everything with its head down gets eaten—chicken, hogs, cows."
Jackie Burke, Jr., on the key to winning

"If we stay ahead every day, I think we'll have a good shot at winning."
Fred Couples, on his strategy at the World Cup with partner Davis Love III

"I guess it gives me another trophy and some crystal and a bunch of money."

Fred Couples, on winning $630,000 at the Players Championship

"You take it when you get it, and right now I'm gettin' it."

Beth Daniel, on a hot streak

"What are you going to do? You give these boys a chance and they don't take it."

Walter Hagen, on posting his fourth PGA championship after Al Espinosa three-putted the last hole

"Indescribably delicious."

Hale Irwin, after winning his third U.S. Open

"I'm not happy with a two-shot win. I want more. I want to demoralize them."

Johnny Miller

"If you're not in position, you can't win."

Jack Nicklaus, on the key to winning big tournaments

"Of course, I can say, individually, I hate them."
Alice Ritzman, nonwinner on the LPGA Tour, on a current group of young stars winning tournaments

"To succeed, you can't be afraid to fail. To win, you've got to put yourself in a position to lose."
Curtis Strange

"If you swing badly but score well and win, don't change a thing."
Lee Trevino

"Great players learn that they don't need to play their best golf to win. They only need to shoot their lowest score."
Tom Watson

"It's kind of funny to see a 6'3" guy who's eight pounds overweight and walks like a duck heading down the fairway with tears in his eyes."
Tom Weiskopf, on what it meant to win the U.S. Seniors Open and beat Jack Nicklaus in the process

"Finally, I'm part of USGA history."
>> *Tom Weiskopf, on his victory at the*
>> *U.S. Senior Open*

WORKING STIFF

"I'd miss it [golf] something terrible, but I could live without it. What scares me the most is that if that happened, I might have to get a real job. That's frightening."
>> *Fuzzy Zoeller, on a*
>> *career-threatening injury*

WORLD TOUR

"We played with the butcher and the baker. In America you never play with the guy with no money."
>> *Steve Elkington, on the difference*
>> *between playing in Australia and the*
>> *United States*

"I call it the Sphinx Links."

> *Robert Trent Jones, on a golf course*
> *he designed near the pyramids*

"Gavea is the toughest course you can imagine. It makes Pine Valley look like a mini. A genius comes along once in 100 years who could break par at Gavea."

> *Gary Player, on shooting a 59*
> *at Gavea Country Club in Rio*
> *de Janeiro*

MICKEY WRIGHT

"I didn't think anybody but the Babe could hit 'em like that."

> *Babe Didrikson, on Mickey Wright at*
> *age 19*

"Mickey Wright was the best female player ever, bar none. And there's not even a second, third, fourth."

> *Dave Marr*

"Mickey got the outside world to take a second look at women golfers, and when they looked they saw the rest of us."

Judy Rankin

"She set a standard of shotmaking that will probably never be equaled."

Betsy Rawls, on Mickey Wright

"It is seriously to be doubted if any woman golfer has ever played a stretch of 36 holes with the power, accuracy, and overall command."

Herbert Warren Wind, on Wright's winning the '61 U.S. Women's Open

INDEX

237